Narcissistic Abuse and Codependency Recovery

Recover from Narcissistic and Codependent
Relationships, Set Strong Boundaries,
Improve Self-Esteem, and End the Toxic
Cycle Forever

Linda Hill

i

Table of Contents

Linda Hill

Your Secret Gift #1:

Get My Next Book

"Narcissistic Abuse and Codependency Recovery - Part 2"

(Free for a limited time)

For a limited time, and as a "Thank you" for purchasing this book, you can be added to our "Book 2 Launch List" for free so you get the second book of this series when it gets published (This book will be priced at $24.99 and I guarantee it will be a great read). Simply visit the URL below and follow the instructions. You'll be the first to get it.

Visit here:

lindahillbooks.com/ncr

Scan QR Code:

Your Secret Gift #2

Get the Audio Version for Free

If you would like to get the audio version of this book so you can read along or listen while you are in the car, walking around, or doing other things, you're in luck. For a limited time, I've provided a link that will allow you to download this audiobook for FREE. (This offer may be removed at any time).

Step 1: Go to the URL below.

Step 2: Sign up for the 30-day free-trial membership (You may cancel at any time after, no strings attached)

Step 3: Listen to the audiobook

Visit here:

lindahillbooks.com/ncrpromo

Scan QR Code:

Introduction

Have you just come out of a relationship with a codependent or narcissistic person? Or, maybe you are wondering if your partner is a codependent or narcissist. Or, perhaps you are past all of that and are trying to figure out how to build a healthy life after a codependent or narcissistic relationship and avoid creating a repeat connection.

The answer to all of those questions comes in the form of healthily recovering from that relationship and its associated trauma (yes, even if you are currently still in that relationship), through broadening your awareness and knowledge about codependents and narcissists, along with yourself.

But how do you do that?

You do that by creating a firm knowledge of understanding about who, what, and how codependents and narcissists work in and out of relationships, plus focusing on ensuring that you as a person, are stronger and more self-aware. Thankfully, this type of knowledge can happen whether you remain with a codependent or narcissistic partner/family member/friend, or not.

However, it should be noted that if at any time throughout this book, you begin to notice dangerous and unhealthy behaviors you do not have to stay, and you most likely should not really stay anyways.

This book was written with the intent of helping you understand, spot, and heal from a codependent or narcissistic relationship. It will neither specifically or directly advocate for you to stay or go. The goal here is to provide you with enough information to make that type of decision on your own.

Before going into the nitty gritty of understanding codependents and narcissists, there are several things you should know. Specifically, terms and a few other notes.

Terms

For some of you, these terms may seem the same from other books and you may want to skip them. While that is your prerogative, it is highly suggested that you read through them to ensure that you understand how these phrases/words have been changed in order to meet the subject matter of this book.

Codependent

According to *Merriam-Webster*, the definition for "codependent" is as follows (n.d.):

> A psychological condition or a relationship in which a person manifesting low self-esteem and a strong desire for approval has an unhealthy attachment to another often controlling or manipulative person (such as a person with an addiction to alcohol or drugs) broadly: dependence on the needs of or on control by another.

What this means is that if your partner was codependent, they may have put their own needs aside in order to ensure that yours, and everyone else's, needs were met. For now, this is a basic understanding of the term codependent, before going into the following chapter.

Narcissistic

The definition for narcissism is: "extremely self-centered with an exaggerated sense of self-importance: marked by or characteristic of excessive admiration of or infatuation with oneself" (Merriam-Webster, n.d.-b). Meaning that signs your partner, friend, or family member may be narcissistic is that they tend to mark down your own accomplishments, feelings, or needs, to over-accentuate their own.

Again, this is a base understanding before going into the first chapter.

Safe Person

For some parts of this book there may be phrases where "safe person" is used. If you are unfamiliar with that term, it will be briefly explained to you here, and feel free to refer to it as you read if need be.

A safe person is someone who you trust implicitly. You tell them every single tiny detail of your life; nothing is too small, too mundane, or too much information. They never judge you, or if they do, it is to gently persuade you to begin rethinking some life choices. They know that what you tell them is for their ears only and it is never repeated or brought up out of context or around other people. They help you realize things you have been quietly thinking about for awhile, but have not told anyone. You never feel unsafe, or non-validated in their presence. Their relationship means a lot to you, and it is cherished.

A good sign that you have a safe person in your life is that you can be completely authentic with them because you know they will never judge you or make you question their respect for you. Safe people take many forms; for some, it could be their parents, mentors, or a friend. However you find them, these people are most likely the ones that have been gently getting you to think about the relationships in your life which are causing you to question if that person is a codependent or narcissist. Essentially, they are most likely that quiet, insistent voice that something is not quite right.

In regard to being in a relationship with a codependent or narcissistic person, your safe people are the ones who will confirm, or help you flesh out, understanding how, where, and why your partner, friend, or family member may be one.

Small Note

It should be noted, however, that just like all of us, our safe people are people as well; meaning that they will make mistakes, and should be allowed to make them. They are not perfect, and will often strive to help you to the best of their ability, but that ability may be limited by knowledge, age, or any combination.

If your safe person has, for whatever reason, made you feel unsafe, take a moment to yourself and think about why you now feel unsafe. If you think that this person is no longer safe for you, then find another confidant. However, if they now feel unsafe for a misstep with you, such as poor wording, or not understanding; think about the conflict and if you feel secure enough, approach them and try to resolve it. Safe people are hard to come by, and they, like us, deserve a second chance if they have proven it.

Additionally, be incredibly discriminatory with who you make a safe person. These people are not just anyone; they have to have knowledge, wisdom and a great amount of understanding and empathy to help be a guiding light and voice of reason in your life. Meaning you most likely should not pick someone you just met to be a safe person. They may grow into one overtime, but part of the reason safe people are who they are is because they actually know you. They have some type of history of your life and an understanding of your quirks, traits, desires, and dreams. Safe people use this knowledge to help guide you and be there for you, and honestly, newfound relationships are not the place this type of knowledge sprouts from immediately.

Accountability Partner

Accountability partners are a big part of the post-addict lifestyle, as they help recovering addicts keep clean. But that does not mean that they cannot be used outside of that circle as well.

Essentially, an accountability partner is someone who you trust implicitly, and who has the right to call you out on the things you do. It may be uncomfortable, it may not be what you want to hear, but the main requirement of an accountability partner is that they call it like they see it; and they will keep bringing it up, until you tell them why that particular action has not happened, or why you do not want to.

Flags

This term refers to a way you can classify certain instances, discussions, or arguments you have with someone, not just your codependent or narcissistic relationship.

Red Flag

This term refers to instances where you need to hit "pause" and really ask yourself why you are still there (in that discussion, relationship, or circumstance). Just like red lights, or red stop signs, red flags in a relationship are signs that you need to stop immediately or very soon in the near future. If you are wondering where the wiggle room is, for this term, there is none. A great equivalent to a red flag would be abuse. The only people who think that that is okay are the abusers. That is all.

If you, or someone you know, is in a red flag situation, make sure that they are aware and that they are somehow able to leave immediately. And safely.

Now, some of you might be thinking, *Whoa, that was way too intense for the first few pages of this book!* and that is true. Welcome to the significance of red flags. They do not always have to be abusive, but they essentially refer to something—and it could be anything—that is unhealthy, dangerous, or really anything you do not want in your life.

In our world there are some things that are always red flags, such as abuse. But you are also encouraged to make your own. For instance, for an ex-alcoholic, this could mean not dating people who are heavy drinkers. You are perfectly allowed to make your own red flags and judge your relationships accordingly.

Small Note

There are going to be a lot of these, so be prepared. While it is perfectly within your right to have red flags that are not "acknowledged" by society as a greater governing board, be prepared that they might rub some people the wrong way or potentially start conflicts. If your red flags are genuine, used sparingly and appropriately, then do not let people challenge you on that. These types of red flags are what we call personal boundaries—which will be briefly discussed here and then defined and more deeply discussed in a later chapter—and should be respected by all.

That being said, if you create arbitrary red flags, change them, and do not respect them yourself, then do not expect others to respect them either. Red flags should neve be used to harm other people or enforce your own will and judgment on others. Doing so makes you no better than the person who harmed you. Instead, red flags are meant to be your mental, emotional, and physical "STOP" sign. It is your get out of jail free card. It is the one thing which will cause you to leave immediately and never look back. However, they should be used sparingly, with high awareness, and also great respect and awareness for the people around you.

So, in sum: A red flag is a big "no" in any type of relationship to the point where you need to stop things and leave. They do not have to be recognized by society en masse, but they do have to be something you can still stick to consistently and that comes from a place of protecting yourself.

Yellow Flag

Ah, the yellow flag. The blessed middle-ground in any relationship. Like a stop light, yellow is the "caution" that can either mean keep going, or to slow down. In relationships, these are generally where we put our own personal spin on what is acceptable, what is not, and what we may let pass for now–but that could change. It is essentially all the fluid "what ifs" in any type of relationship, which could change in an instant.

For example, many yellow flags exist in young or casual relationships (or at the start of one). It is something you are currently unsure of, and want to put on hold to make a stronger opinion or decision about later. Often they end up resolving themselves by either upgrading to a red flag, or downgrading to a green flag.

In any type of relationship, the yellow flag is where we tend to create, share, and enforce our personal boundaries. They are in the yellow category because they may not be for everybody, or you may still be unsure about how you feel regarding that particular trait, instance, or boundary.

Green Flag

These do not really need explaining. These are the things that make any relationship great and are usually the reason the relationship starts and/or continues.

Personal Boundaries

Ah, the long-awaited personal boundaries. Remember, these will be discussed in a later chapter. For now, think of personal boundaries similar to a property line of a house. It is a line that you, and others around you, work to maintain, and everyone knows how they relate to that line.

For example: your neighbor knows not to cross that line unless invited. The city does no work past that line, and you decide who can, or cannot, come in.

It is as simple as that.

Other Notes

Here we will briefly go over a few other things to know before you continue to read this book. The first is that nowhere in this book, are you meant to feel personally accountable, or demeaned for your situation. That is absolutely not what this book is intended for.

However, there will also be times where you will be called to task. Just like any relationship—even unhealthy ones—there are still times when the victim has to be made accountable for their own actions. In this book, what that will mean is acknowledging to yourself and either a: safe person, therapist, counselor, and/or accountability partner, what you personally did wrong in that situation. Nowhere in here is it necessarily recommended you say these things to your partner, so do not worry about it, unless you are in a specific situation (but this will be discussed in a later chapter). What it does mean is that you will be forced to grow personal accountability and self-awareness, through the use of hindsight.

The other note that you should be aware of is having a journal, or person to talk to, while you read this book. It is so easy to have that "Aha!" moment while reading, and then two seconds later you have completely forgotten it. When it comes to reading fiction, this is completely fine, because you most likely will have remembered enough to continue the plot. But for these types of self-help books, where you are going to be doing the majority of introspective work on your own, it is highly recommended that you keep a journal beside/with this book, so that you can write down those moments as they come to you.

These little breakthroughs need to be recorded so that you can later re-read and reflect on them. Because it is in those moments of reflection where your true personal growth and recovery will start.

CHAPTER 1

The Narcissistic and Codependent: Same Needs, Different Behaviors

Now that we have an understanding of what you need to know for this book, it is time to actually begin discussing codependents and narcissists. Starting with why they were grouped together. There are many times where it is not that difficult to differentiate between codependent and narcissistic behaviors; in fact, some could argue that it is harder to find similarities than differences. However, when it comes to identifying which category you may be dealing with in your own life, it is not enough to simply recognize which category someone falls into; you also need to begin understanding their needs and behaviors.

All humans have needs, and all of these needs are shown through different types of behaviors; but sometimes, our needs are actually the same, yet we present them differently. For instance, take toddlers. One may cry when he wants food, while another may simply ask for it. The need for food is the same, but how they go about getting that food is incredibly different. While this may seem like a gross oversimplification of the concept, the principle is the same.

Codependent and narcissistic people behave differently, but they often have the same needs. However, before we can truly begin understanding these similarities and differences, you need a firm understanding of what codependent and narcissistic people look like; because while you may be dealing with one in your personal life, they are not the only ones out there and everyone behaves a little bit differently.

To help you get a firm grasp on the similarities and differences between a codependent and narcissist, this chapter will be divided into two main sections to discuss each mental state. Each section will then discuss the textbook traits of both psychological states, as well as begin to discuss their separate needs and associated behaviors.

Codependency

What It Is

In case you do not remember the exact definition of a

codependent, according to *Merriam-Webster*, a codependent is (n.d.):

> a psychological condition or a relationship in which a person manifesting low self-esteem and a strong desire for approval has an unhealthy attachment to another often controlling or manipulative person (such as a person with an addiction to alcohol or drugs) broadly: dependence on the needs of or on control by another.

Notice something within the definition? Look at the phrase: "dependence on the needs of or on control by another" (Merriam-Webster, n.d.). Codependents are essentially unable to define their self-worth on their own, it has to be done through other people (Martin, 2020). Which in turn, often makes them high people pleasers. Sadly, this characteristic makes it hard to spot codependents immediately, since being people-pleasers gives them a chameleon-like ability to hide in plain sight within social events and situations.

That is, until you get into a relationship with them.

So, in sum: a codependent gains their self-identity by putting the needs of others before their own, making them the ultimate people pleasers in a group and also social chameleons.

How It Came to Be

While the upcoming chapter will go more in-depth into this

discussion, it needs to begin here. Codependents–like narcissists–often come from a place of abuse. However, unlike narcissists, codependents learn their codependent ways through witnessing it first-hand from someone within their immediate circle and by adapting to the experienced abuse differently (Utti et al., 2016).

By learning these behaviors as a way to avoid the conflict of their traumatic past–whenever that happened–and as a conjoined action to begin finding and fostering love, our codependent person is "born."

The Needs

When it comes to the need, codependents are very simple: they want to feel loved and needed by those around them; particularly their innermost circle such as romantic partners, friends, family members, and even immediate coworkers. In each of these relationships, a codependent person will put the needs of the other person above their own.

Now, let's peel back a codependent's need to an even deeper level. Because they need to be needed, this can become a really dangerous and unhealthy cycle of self-denial (literally) and lead to the mental pathway of people pleaser, to enabler, to controller and manipulator to "help" someone. Seems odd, right? How could that even happen?

Because codependents let someone else's desires affect them to the point where they become obsessed with controlling everything—including that person—to get that outcome. Considering that codependents often pick emotionally unavailable, abusive, and/or addictive people as their partners already, this creates an unhealthy and dangerous cycle which still centers upon a codependent's innermost need of needing to be needed.

Being the main instigator and architect of someone else's life or "thing," such a someone's sobriety journey, will give codependents their ultimate sense of fulfillment. Or, so they think.

The Problem

Whenever someone gives up an intrinsic need in any type of relationship, there is already a big red flag of a problem. However, compound onto that an even deeper intrinsic problem with codependents: they often do not feel worthy of love or affection, which causes them to go into loveless and emotionally unavailable romantic relationships or friendships (Utti et al., 2016).

While it may seem odd, to a codependent, it is this weird give and take. They give up their needs and wants to ultimately serve the other person, and they will eventually get feelings of love, security, and value in return. Notice the problem within the problem? Actually, there are two. First, codependents give up and ignore their own needs and wants (or boundaries) which is never healthy. Second, they believe that their actions can change and cause another person—who is completely autonomous and most likely not aware of this plan—to love them back. Healthy relationships never work this way. Partners consistently choose to love the other, regardless of their actions.

Which brings up the next problem: this usually does not end up happening, due to who codependents tend to pick to be in their inner circle, particularly, as romantic partners.

It is not enough for a codependent person to be helpful, they need to be the key to your success, your reason to continue trying, and the main motivation behind how you work and why you are doing something. On the one hand, this may seem quite positive and perhaps even endearing. And that is how it can present itself, at first.

As some of you might have guessed, everything that has been discussed so far is a glaring sign of no personal boundaries, and this is another key identifier of a codependent person. While there will be another chapter entirely devoted to boundaries, it is important to say this here: if you have to give up your sense of self, mental health, physical health, and/or emotional health in order to feel validated and wanted in a relationship: you are exhibiting no personal boundaries.

Additionally, exhibiting no boundaries, along with needing to be needed, brings up another problem of a codependent person: they actually struggle with imperfection, specifically their own. This may seem like an odd leap to take, but take a moment to think about it: a personal boundary is accepting what you are and are not responsible for in your own life, and what/how other people can affect your own, *along* with how you can, or cannot, affect someone else's life.

That was a mouthful, so let's go over that again: A personal boundary is understanding what you will let others do, or not do, to/in your own life—as well as you understanding what you can, or cannot do, in someone else's life.

Therefore, having healthy boundaries includes accepting what you are, or are not, capable of. Especially your imperfections such as: your inability to time manage, keep a clean house, or remember to text someone back. However, accepting imperfections through a deep sense of self-awareness, personal boundaries, and forgiveness and acceptance; are things that codependents subconsciously shy away from.

Not only is that type of scenario uncomfortable to a healthy person, to a codependent person that is like walking into a ballroom full of professional dancers naked and expected to dance with them. Accepting that they are imperfect, and therefore, cannot be everything their partner intrinsically needs (remember, we are discussing uncharacteristically high needs that should never be put on a person in the first place) is one of the biggest fears a codependent can have.

And they are going to hide those fears, recognizing that they (the codependent) cannot be everything and are imperfect, through refusing their own needs, by being everything their partner—or anyone else—could ever ask for.

Which is ironic, because, in actuality, they are putting their needs above their partner's, by using their partner's needs as their own.

What It Looks Like

While understanding what codependency is has probably painted a pretty good mental image of what/how it could appear (or is appearing) in your life, there is still more to it. You now need to begin to understand what codependency looks like on a broad scale. To get a better understanding of how this can look, the manifestations are actually going to be divided into: emotions and then physical actions.

Emotions

Because codependency can hide itself so well at the first couple of instances, it is hard to know what you are dealing with immediately. So, now it is time to actually look into how codependents manifest and express their needs and feelings in a relationship. Particularly when it comes to their feelings and expressions of emotions such as: fear/anxiety, resentment, guilt, and shame.

Essentially, for every emotion that was just listed, think of ways to say, "I am not safe," and that is what codependents will often begin to use. Therefore:

- Resentment often manifests in sayings like: "You should be the way I want you to be."

- Guilt is often more in the enabler category, where they are unable to say no out of the wish to not feel bad about denying someone something.

- Shame comes from their belief that they are not worthwhile or loveable.

Because codependents do not have their own personal boundaries the emotional side of the relationship can get exhausting incredibly fast. Again, this is because everything will be put onto their partner, including the responsibility of their emotions. On the other hand, this also means that partners of codependents will find it incredibly easy to take advantage of, or dismiss, their partner (the codependents) wants or needs. Especially since they will often not verbalize them to the same extent a healthy or even narcissistic person would. In fact, you would be lucky if they verbalized their wants at all.

Actions

When it comes to actions, remember: codependents need to feel their partner needing them, and they gain their feelings of love and acceptance through those actions. This means that the actions of a codependent could actually come off as incredibly loving and attentive at first.

The honeymoon stage of dating is when any of us lavish our partner in our form of love and affection. It is only when we begin to get to know the person that we actually know what they will prefer and what makes them feel loved. For a codependent, both of these stages are relatively "easy" because they will go along with whatever you think they would want.

Small Note

Now, there is an incredibly fine line between understanding your partner's best wishes—even if that is not your desire—and being a codependent who will take any form of affection as long as it is what their partner wants.

In a relationship, it is normal at times to accept tokens of love from your partner which are not your specific love language. This may even continue into a long-term committed relationship. You accept small and occasional tokens of your partner's love language for you, because you know that they love you.

23

Here is a great example: Alex loves the color purple, so his wife Jane wears it often because she knows he loves it, even though she is not the biggest fan of that color. However, it does not harm her, or push any of her own personal boundaries. On the other side, Alex will often wear green because it is Jane's favorite color.

In this example, Alex and Jane wear things they know their partner intrinsically likes, because it makes their partner happy. However, neither of their actions are hurting the other, crossing personal boundaries, or putting the other in danger. It is simply acknowledging what their partner likes and working within that sphere occasionally.

A codependent relationship will not do that. Specifically: the codependent person will always do something that their partner will love, whereas the partner will be operating on a surface-level (or perhaps off of lies) from what they have not been told.

The Behaviors

Now onto the specific behaviors of a codependent. Actions and behaviors are slightly different. At the risk of being a grammar geek, an action is a verb. Meaning it is the actual act that a person will do to showcase emotions, feelings, or behaviors. In comparison, a behavior is a noun, meaning that it is a mindset or way something is done.

In this case, the behaviors of codependents so far are relatively straightforward from what we have talked about so far: They are people pleasers, and they need you to need them.

However, there are other behaviors which have not yet been discussed. Unfortunately, the ones that are about to come up are the less than fun side of codependents and point to a lot of negatives that people who are in relationships with them can experience. These include:

- The repression of their own feelings, wants, or desires

- Obsessive thinking

- Controlling

- Often in denial—cannot see that they are allowing the problem to continue

- Poor communicators; they cannot say or even completely know how they feel

- Weak boundaries

- Lack of trust

- Anger

- Sexual problems

And "best" but not least, these types of problems, traits, or symptoms, appear whether they are in a relationship or not. On the one hand, this is good, because if you are careful, you may begin to notice who is potentially codependent or not, without ever getting into a close relationship with them. On the other hand, none of the things in the above list are fun to deal with once you are actually in close proximity to them.

Narcissistic

What It Is

As seen in the introduction, the definition of narcissism is: "extremely self-centered with an exaggerated sense of self-importance: marked by or characteristic of excessive admiration of or infatuation with oneself" (Merriam-Webster, n.d.-b).

While that is not hard to understand, just to be completely crystal clear, this means that compared to codependents, narcissists are obsessed with themselves to the point of this obsession coming at the cost of their attention-span and willingness to acknowledge other people.

This does not mean that narcissists are unable to form relationships, or ignore other people entirely. What this really is referring to is their emotional inability to put others ahead of themselves, or even being willing to let the spotlight leave them for very long.

There is another incredibly important differential between codependents and narcissists: narcissism is actually a recognized personality disorder called narcissistic personality disorder (NPD) (Kassel, 2022). In reality, this recognition does very little, especially when it comes to how to deal with a narcissist. However it does mean that there are more specific treatments and resources dealing with narcissism.

How It Came to Be

Similar to codependents, narcissists often have childhood or past traumas with abuse. However, unlike codependents, narcissists adapted to that abuse differently. While this will be covered in a later chapter (literally the next one), it is important to begin getting this common ground into general knowledge. Plus, having a brief understanding of how narcissists are created will help you begin to put the rest of this chapter into perspective.

The Needs

Where codependents only seem simple on the surface, narcissists are pretty self-explanatory from the moment they are noted as a narcissist. Their need is to be the "it" in the room. This "it" is generally very specific to the narcissist themselves, but a great way to look at it is they have to be the biggest and the best at whatever situation/environment they are in. Normally, narcissism tends to encompass all areas of someone's life, but it is possible for it to center only on certain areas.

What this need means, however, is that narcissists ultimately care too much about what others think about them, and they actually begin to base their identity and self-worth off of that (Villines, 2018). Which can create problems over time. Think about it for a minute: If a narcissist believes that they are the best at whatever it is, then they need the rest of the room to believe that, too. Ergo, the minute someone doubts, or worse, proof comes up that they are no longer the biggest and best one in "x" category, the narcissist is going to do almost anything in their power to have that spot back.

What It Looks Like

Spotting a narcissist is often not too difficult, however there is a fine line between someone who is perhaps overly confident and a narcissist. Basically, if someone is able to back up their claims to greatness or abilities, then they are confident. If they brag about it consistently, but they are still right, then they are overly confident. Narcissists will make themselves seem more important than they are, and will often not have the same level of abilities to back up their claims.

Here are some other attributes that narcissists may have,

according to *BetterHelp* (2022):

- They will feel and overstate their importance in any type of dynamic/setting.

- They will often have fantasies about how important they are. These fantasies may be attached to a mythical or historical figure they believe they are aligned with somehow.

- They will believe that they are special or unique. As a special note for this one: this particular trait is not a defining characteristic of narcissists. People who are insecure in themselves will also often create a fictitious belief that they are more important to 'x' than they actually are. However, this point is a great concluding argument as to why someone may be a narcissist.

- They have an incredibly high need to be constantly recognized and praised. Again, as a note: Many of us perform better when we are praised for accomplishments we have actually earned. That is normal and healthy. When it comes to narcissists, they will charm and suck up to those around them to get that praise, rather than work for it.

- They come off as condescending and entitled.

- They tend to exploit others to take the credit, which then helps inflate their sense of importance or need to be flattered and admired.

- They have a lack of empathy. For people with narcissistic personality disorder, this is an actual lack of ability within their brains; it is not that they do not want to empathize (although that may also be true), but they often are actually incapable of doing so.

- They have an almost paranoid sense of envy; someone is always jealous of them, or they are always jealous of someone else.

- They are often arrogant and haughty. Narcissists will talk down to anyone they feel is beneath them, which is basically everyone.

- They are sensitive to criticism or defeat. Narcissists tend to be incredibly poor losers. They will often react to criticism or defeat by blaming others, becoming disproportionately angry, or even withdrawing from the situation entirely.

- They don't have as big of a social circle. When you think about it, it makes sense. Most of the traits of a narcissist are not incredibly endearing in the long-term for someone who has healthy personal boundaries. So often, narcissists will rise and fall in popularity due to who they are able to maintain within their circle and those who will leave.

- They have a fear of failure and an unwillingness to take risks. Because narcissists thrive—and need—to maintain their sense of perfection throughout every part of their lives, it makes sense that they are unable and unwilling to shatter that image by taking a risk that could end in failure.

The Behaviors

Remember: Behaviors are essentially the mindsets for the actions. Therefore, for a narcissist the mindsets are relatively simple: it is to fulfill their lack of identity by being the best, the most, or whatever "it" is, in that specific setting.

Example

James was always an incredibly nice guy at work. He complimented everyone and was easy to get along with. Fiona noticed this and soon the two began talking. However, as the couple's relationship progressed, James noticed that Fiona had stopped reciprocating the nice gestures—particularly the compliments and special actions at work—that she had done at the beginning of their relationship. Whenever the couple went out to dinner Fiona always had to hog the conversation and would pout when James did not compliment her outfit or eagerly destroy another woman's outfit/look to make her feel better.

About six months into the relationship, James was miserable and feeling ignored.

There are several things to notice here. First: Fiona was charming at first. In order to gain an audience, or a partner, narcissists instinctively know that they need to give as good as they get in order for someone to stay. However, once they are confident in the relationship or situation, that charming personality will no longer be as prevalent. Second, Fiona could not handle someone being better looking than her and she made sure James had the same mindset. Third, Fiona had to always be the center of attention. She insisted that she be the one always talking, and did not reciprocate or make James feel included in the conversation. He had become her audience, not her partner.

The Same but Not

Then, the final section will discuss the combined needs of both codependents and narcissists, while pointing out their different behaviors, to help you get a better perspective on how this may look in your own life.

Essentially, the main similarity between codependents and narcissists is that they both lack a sense of personal identity through themselves. Instead, they rely on others to fuel and give them that identity through their different ways of getting it

(Villines, 2018).

When it comes to codependents, they will forget themselves in order to make their partner/someone else happy—and make *that* happiness their identity and sense of self and self-fulfillment.

In comparison, narcissists will use the praise and good will of others—earned or not—to make themselves seem more important than they actually are. Overtime, or even immediately, their actions will come at the cost of someone else.

Journaling

Now comes the interpersonal moment for this chapter. Take a moment with your journal or recording device, and begin to think about where and how you experienced any of the situations listed in this chapter. Your experiences do not have to fully line up with the examples, but the general idea should be the same.

While you are writing down these moments, make sure that you list everything: the date, the time, the place, how those conversations came up, how you reacted, how you felt then, how you feel now, their reaction, and the reaction/emotions/input of those around (if it was in a public setting).

The goal is to help you gain awareness so that you can begin to notice these types of things as they happen, instead of needing hindsight to even get your brain to make the connection.

CHAPTER 2

The Common Ground of Adverse Childhood Experiences

While the previous chapter pointed out similarities between codependents and narcissists, we will now delve more deeply into those commonalities in this chapter. Hopefully by understanding how codependents and narcissists are similar through their childhood experiences, you will begin to get a better understanding of how and why they are who they are.

Small Note

At the end of the day, knowing how and why your partner or person is a codependent or narcissist can only go so far. While it is great knowledge for you to have so that you can begin formulating and figuring out exactly what type of trauma and actions you need to be careful of in the future, there is something you should know. Knowing and understanding who and how they came to be is not going to help them in any way.

Unless they are going on this journey with you—and that should be done only in extremely accountable situations where therapists and accountability partners are on both sides—they are not going to change unless they want to.

You have to be doing this journey for you. You have to want to understand them to protect and heal yourself. Not them. People only change when they want to, and if they were unwilling to change themselves before, it is unlikely that they will want to change themselves now.

Also, this book was written to help guide you and help you make your own choices. Anything that is said in this chapter, a previous one, or upcoming chapters, are in no way a diagnosis or statement saying that you or someone you know is definitely a codependent or narcissist. That is impossible to conclude from simply writing about codependency/narcissism and never meeting you, the reader, or hearing about the situation/scenarios.

If you feel that you might be codependent or narcissistic, or if you believe you are in a relationship with one, find a licensed professional (such as a therapist or counselor) and they will help determine if you/they are, or are not.

So as you go forward with this chapter, remember: these are general guidelines and notes to begin noticing/acknowledging if someone you know is codependent or narcissistic. It is not a diagnosis and should not be treated as such.

Alright, so now that those little tidbits are out of the way, it is time to discuss the similarities of narcissists and codependents, specifically how they came to be.

Unfortunately, both behaviors tend to stem from a background or childhood of abuse (Villines, 2018). This is not always true for every single one, and someone who experiences childhood abuse may not become a codependent or narcissist. However, there is an uncanny correlation between the two in regard to emotional neglect (which is a form of abuse), and how the children of this type of abuse have an interesting relationship with their sense of self (Villines, 2018). What causes a child to become a codependent or narcissist is essentially how they choose to adapt to that abuse as they age (Villines, 2018).

A great way to look at it is that:

- Codependents are formed due to low self-esteem and believe that they must earn someone's affection.

- Narcissists create a self-protective mechanism of essentially pretending they do not need anyone else's input, which is all they want and desire in reality.

As a warning, this chapter may be a bit triggering to read, so if it is a bit much for you, take some time between reading and finishing the chapter. If you need to, call a friend or therapist, or write down your thoughts and feelings in a safe and secure journal. While it will hurt to read and understand, we can only begin to heal once we acknowledge what has happened, our part, what is not our fault (like their abuse), and how to move on.

So, without further ado, here we go.

The Role of Abuse

As said before, codependents and narcissists are generally a result of childhood, or general, abuse. Abuse occurs in many forms and the scars it leaves are long-lasting (Menter, 2013). For this chapter, the two "main types" of abuse which will be discussed are either negligent and emotionally unavailable parents, or parents who are addicted to something. These are by no means the only types of abuse which could create a codependent or narcissistic person; they are merely the two that are being discussed here.

In the case of codependent and narcissistic people, the type of abuse that is generally experienced is either neglect or scenarios where the child is forced to become the parent due to their parents' inability to fulfill that role (Villines, 2018). Which in turn, is often related to forms of addiction, although that does not have to be an associated factor. Unfortunately, parents can be emotionally neglectful all on their own, but the presence of an addict does not help matters.

Possible Manifestations

When it comes to examining or recounting abuse in the life of the potential codependent or narcissistic person in your own life, there are several ways it might embody itself, according to J.E. Menter:

- Their abusers were parents, siblings, relatives, strangers or peers.

- The abuse was verbal, physical, emotional, or sexual.

- They do not see themselves as abused.

- They are unable to feel genuine happiness.

- Their feelings are easily hurt.

- They are unable to create feelings of trust in anyone.

- They isolate often in order to cope with their trauma.

- They have low self-esteem.

- When life is going well, victims of abuse become uncomfortable and will create chaos, because that is what is "comfortable" to them.

- Victims experience mental confusion: their feelings get mixed up, they experience numbness, or become out of touch with their emotions.

- They often feel dirty, embarrassed, out of control, secretive, or appear guilty.

- They might develop compulsive behaviors such as: over eating, drinking, sex, smoking, etc.

- They will often seek out abusive relationships.

- They will experience violent dreams and flashbacks.

- They will take on the "victim" personality. Please note that there is a big difference between a victim and victim personality. While this will be more fully fleshed out in a later chapter, for here it is enough to recognize that a victim is a victim. However, when someone makes their victim situation the reason they are unable to do anything or get better, it slowly becomes their personality. Which is never a good place to be.

- They may have suicidal or homicidal tendencies, which can occur when past abuse was severe enough and not resolved (Menter, 2013).

The Traits

While this list is incredibly helpful when it comes to hindsight perspective (such as suddenly connecting the dots between some interesting childhood stories you heard while dating, to experiences you now unfortunately have), there are a few common ways to see if you, or someone you know, experienced these things.

Each of these traits will be discussed so that you will be able to further identify which your partner/person you know may have, as well as to help you begin to notice and identify these reactions to trauma earlier on so that you may be able to come up with better exit or coping strategies.

Childhood Immaturity

Survivors of childhood abuse often present a child-like sense of immaturity. It may be sporadic or consistent throughout their social interactions, it all depends on how they have adapted from the abuse as an adult. However, sooner or later, certain signs of childhood immaturity will become noticeable if that person has not gone through intensive therapy about their traumatic experiences.

If you are wondering if you, or your partner, display any sign of childhood immaturity, ask yourself these questions:

- Do you, or they, have an addiction?

- Do you, or they, repress feelings out of a fear of punishment or rejection?

- Were you, or they, abused?

- Do you, or they, feel shame, guilt, anxiety, ignored, fear, or belittled when there is adversity in a conversational/social setting?

- Do you, or they, have low self-esteem?

- Do you, or they, have obsessive behavior?

- Do you, or they, have sexual issues (such as an inability to reach orgasm, or to find someone sexually appealing?)

- Do you, or they, have a record of dysfunctional relationships with parents/caregivers/people in authority?

- Do you, or they, act overly responsible (or controlling) when it is not necessary?

- Do you, or they, have depression?

- Is there a lack of boundaries?

- Do you, or they, obsessively worry over things that are not in any way controllable, or even what you, or they, should be worrying about?

- Do you, or they, feel responsible for your/their caretaker's feelings and well-being, to the point where your/their own needs are no longer necessary or noted?

If you, or they, answered "yes" to any of these questions then there is a sign that somewhere along the line, you or the person you know, are displaying childhood immaturity in certain scenarios, or within your/their life.

Now, before getting all defensive, this is not something that is necessarily your fault. Children have to develop survival mechanisms in an abusive or neglectful household; when the abuse or neglect is gone, these mechanisms are no longer useful. But just because the abuse/neglect has stopped, does not mean that you/they know how to turn those mechanisms off (Peterson, 2018).

Being aware that you, or they, present certain characteristics of childhood immaturity is simply something to take note of and to begin working through either in the following chapters, or with a therapist/counselor.

Amnesia

In this context, "amnesia" is referring to the splitting, or disassociation, of the child/inner child. Children of abuse/neglect develop a mechanism which allows them to mentally check out when they are uncomfortable or in situations where their abuse is present. This allows them to no longer feel the pain and terror they experienced in their childhood (Peterson, 2018).

This reaction can happen to any abuse victim/survivor; but when it comes to child survivors this is especially dangerous, as it has the ability to lead to patterns of behavior. These patterns actually become incredibly harmful to a child's emotional maturity. Say that a child has learned to dissociate, or find a way to create a type of amnesia in certain situations where they are uncomfortable. Now put that type of behavior and mechanism on top of any type of discomfort including natural biological discomforts like: puberty, school dances, young relationships, sharing feelings, healthy forms of confrontation or criticism, etc.

People who come from healthy childhood homes do not think about it once those awkward moments have passed; but each of those instances are incredibly uncomfortable, awkward, and require a high-level of vulnerability to get through. Once you are on the other side of those experiences, however, you have developed a type of maturity, understanding, and knowledge that only going through those experiences can give you.

Now think about what would happen when someone avidly avoids or ignores their emotions during those types of instances. Unfortunately, developing this type of amnesia or dissociation—while necessary to protect themselves—is a heavy factor in why childhood abuse survivors display so many constant forms of childhood immaturity. It is pretty impossible to develop a type of maturity when you expressly avoid those situations. Yet ironically, children from those situations will display strong maturity in other scenarios. So it is not consistent, making it hard to notice at first.

Before going forward it is important to note that how dissociation or amnesia happens or presents itself is incredibly specific to the child/person. They may not avoid all types of awkward emotional encounters, or, they may force themselves to attempt to experience them once they are away from their abusers and in society as a teenager or young adult. This does not mean that they do not dissociate at all—again, that is incredibly specific to the person—but the instances may be rarer than this section has led you to believe.

For this particular trait what you need to begin looking for and notice is when and why your partner, or person you know, dissociates. Signs of dissociation could be: not paying attention in incredibly emotional or confrontational settings, physically walking away, or being unable to be in those types of situations without some type of self-medication, or even just constant self-medication or distractions (like social media or technology).

Loss of Self

Children of abuse tend to lose their sense of identity because their caregivers were abusive and/or neglectful. When we are young, our sense of identity and self-worth come from our caregivers: how they care for us, how present they are, and how they praise us. If a child grows up in a home where that is not present—or it is incredibly circumstantial—then the child will begin to form feelings of worthlessness and discouragement in relation to their sense of self (Peterson, 2018).

Additionally, if someone is from a background of addiction, this sense of self becomes even more distorted. People who live in addiction filled homes do not know what emotional stability looks like, because everything in their house is dictated by the highs and lows of the addict. This means that any type of emotion which is exhibited is volatile, and most of the time, ingenuine. While an addict may feel actual love, happiness, or anger, people—especially children—note when that emotion is due to a substance rather than from within yourself.

This results in a child who is used to living in a world that is dominated by automatic emotional responses, which is an incredibly different mindset from a healthy household, where children display balance between emotions and intellect. People from a non-addictive household know the difference between their emotions and intellect (mindset), and are able to distinguish and display authentic and appropriate emotions. Additionally, these people will be able to make decisions and cope with stress more easily (this is not to say that they will not feel it at all, but they will most likely be able to hold it together, or find better solutions more quickly). They are also more independent (Menter, 2013).

In comparison, someone from an addiction filled, or abusive, home, will not know how to display these emotions genuinely; they will do so out of an automatic response from years of bowing to someone's expectations of demands. Neither will they be able to handle decision making or stress, well, as they have had years experience of handling these emotions continuously in an unstable and unencouraging environment (Menter, 2013).

When someone is in an environment where they are unable to begin creating healthy emotions and reactions, plus an environment where their sense of self is never encouraged, acknowledged, or even discussed, it is no wonder that they have a loss of self. According to Mental Health America, some characteristics of codependency due to a loss of self include the following (Menter, 2013):

- A strong and overemphasized sense of responsibility for the actions of others

- A tendency to muddle love and pity, resulting in "loving" people they pity, so that they can be the hero and rescue that person

- The inclination to constantly do more than their share, even in the little things

- An extreme dependence on relationships, to the point where they will do anything to keep and hold onto a relationship (normally resulting from a deep desire to avoid feeling abandoned)

- The enormous and constant need for approval and recognition

- The need to constantly take control of others and numerous situations

- A strong lack of trust in themselves and in others

- An inability to identify feelings or to "know themselves" confidently

- The display of intense rigidity or difficulty when adjusting to change

- Poor communication skills

- Experience constant difficulty in making decisions

Now, before going further it is important to note that these are traits attributed to codependency and narcissism, and showcasing several at a time would be a good indicator that you might be/know someone who is either of those.

On the other hand, if you have only one or two of these traits, do not worry. There is a good chance you are not codependent or narcissistic (again, this is not a diagnosis or absolute saying either way), this is merely pointing out that if you noticed some tendencies, become more in tune with yourself (which we will discuss in a future chapter) before making a direct decision or taking action.

Violence and Neglect

Unfortunately, violence and neglect are trade-mark characteristics of abusive households. The violence and neglect do not necessarily have to come out directly onto the child, however, it could present itself in violence towards animals or inanimate objects, or the neglect could present itself as the parent doing the absolute bare-minimum requirements, but not emotionally connecting with their child.

When it comes to homes with addiction, violence and neglect are unfortunately present and are displayed in the ways most people would expect. One study done in three major metropolitan areas revealed that 78% of cases in which children were put into foster care involved substance abuse by the parents (Menter, 2013). When it comes to the children of these homes, not only are they desensitized to these actions, but they may also begin using them as their own form of coping tools and desperate attempts to gain control back over their own lives. Which means that when it comes to being a partner of a codependent or narcissistic person, you may actually begin to experience these actions yourself. Again, it may not be towards you directly, but it is still something to watch out for.

No one should ever be in a home where they experience violence or neglect, even if it is indirect; the same goes for a partner of a childhood abuse survivor. Just because they were able to bravely survive their childhood does not mean that you deserve a repeat of what they experienced.

However, what this also means is that the survivor may not be entirely sure that they are doing it. Yes, most people are pretty aware when they punch someone, but when it comes to being emotionally neglectful, someone may be unaware that that is what they are doing (but that is not always the case). This is in no way a justification for someone's actions. It is merely pointing out that both violence and neglect may actually become a coping mechanism of someone who experienced those actions towards themselves.

Emotional Damage

It almost goes without saying, but children who grew up in addictive or abusive households leave those homes with emotional damage. This damage could present itself in a multitude of ways, some of which we have already discussed. However another aspect of this emotional damage is the permanent implantation of negative feelings. These include:

anger, hate, guilt, fear, blame, and shame.

Part of the reason they have these emotions is because they instinctively know that this home life is not normal, natural, or even healthy. When anyone is in a situation they know is completely not natural and messed up, they experience feelings of anger, hate, guilt, fear, blame, and shame. We see it all the time in modern films, TV shows, books, etc., when characters are displaced into events and situations that are not normal. The problem is that children of abuse have these feelings long after the abuse has finished; and these emotions often come out disproportionately to triggering situations (Peterson, 2018). What triggers a child will really depend on their specific experiences with abuse; however, if you or your partner, or someone you know, reacts disproportionately with any of the abovementioned emotions to certain situations, that is a pretty good indicator that there is past trauma.

When it comes to children who suffered an addiction filled childhood, these emotions may transfer into other areas, such as finances and familial roles. On the surface, this may seem a little odd and maybe even arbitrary, so let's walk through it quickly. Addiction in a childhood home often means that one parent or caregiver, maybe even both, are addicts. Traditionally, addicts become distant and non-participants in the lives around them, either because they are currently on the high of whatever substance they use, or are on a depression-filled withdrawal (yes, this is a bit of an oversimplification of the addiction process, but bear with it for a moment). In either scenario, the spouse— if they are not an addict—plays the uncomfortable and draining role of being both an enabler to their spouse and super-parent to their shared children.

Children are smart. They pick up on when someone is drained, tired, or frustrated, no matter how hard someone tries to hide it. Which makes it even more frustrating for the child when the other parent suffers more than the addicted parent, during their childhood. On top of that, because one parent is often left to be everything to the entire family, the older children will either step-up—or be made to step-up—as a pseudo parent and caregiver to their addicted parent/caregiver, as well as their younger siblings (Menter, 2013).

And that is just discussing the familial role emotional damage a child of abuse suffers from. When it comes to finances, children of abuse or addiction are well aware money is not something that is easy to come by. Either this is because the addict/self-absorbed parent will spend it all on themselves, and save very little for their children. Or, the other spouse/caregiver has to hide money to provide for their family, and lie to their spouse/partner in order to do that. Additionally, if the child is put into a pseudo-caregiver role, part of that role will be them lying and hiding the money as well.

No wonder children of abuse and addiction have emotional

trauma, as well as weird relationships with familial roles and money.

Wacky Boundaries

As with almost anything addiction or abuse touches, any type of boundary which may be present in a home with addiction goes from one extreme to another.

On the one end, relationships are squashed together, meaning that individuals are too close and it is almost impossible to create a true sense of self. Anything that is different is not allowed and there is an emphasis on over-responsibility for each other's feelings and identities. The family/household takes on this extreme sense of "we" which ensures that developing minds and identities are unable—and maybe even scared—to fully accept or acknowledge that they are in fact, an individual (Menter, 2013).

This type of extreme boundary will often present itself in situations where children are not allowed to pull away or become autonomous. They are never encouraged to pursue their own talents, interests, etc., or to develop any type of extraordinary pursuits, talents, or intellect. In adult relationships—any type of adult relationship—people who grew up with this type of lack of boundary will often give up their sense of identity for the sake of keeping the peace (Menter, 2013).

On the other end of the spectrum, abuse and addiction households could create distant relationships with little intimacy or familiarity between members. These homes experience little to no sharing of emotions or express any desire or attempt to connect between each other, creating feelings of isolation and an unhealthy sense of individuality, more like the lone wolf, or lone island. In some situations, the entire family isolates from the community (Menter, 2013).

In either circumstance, these types of boundaries create an adult who either does not know how to define themselves outside of an unhealthily close community, or how to connect with anyone at all.

Rules

Just like with boundaries, children who grow up in a home filled with abuse or addiction experience extreme rules. On the one side, there is a form of rigidity that is almost unparalleled within the home. Spoken and unspoken rules exist to protect and work around the addiction or abuse rather than the family. Or, on the other side, there are virtually no rules, and the children are left to raise themselves (Menter, 2013).

Normally, rules in an addiction or abuse filled home have the same three rules, regardless of whatever else there is. First: talking about the abuse or addiction is forbidden, even within the home. Second, do not trust. Third, do not feel. Part of the reason these rules exist is because generally, addicts can only show affection, such as anger or happiness, when they are using. The rest of the time, they wish to be left alone (Menter, 2013). Which is why these rules are in place.

If you are unsure if you understand, or if your childhood falls into any of those three rules, let's go through some examples.

The first rule is: Talking about addiction is forbidden, even in the home. When an addict is not using, they are generally upset and/or experiencing withdrawals, making even talking about the substance a painful reminder of what they do not have. Additionally, this rule might even spill over into other "forbidden" substances. For instance, if the child is growing up in a drug-based home, they may also be forbidden to discuss or talk about alcohol, since that could be the addict's back-up for withdrawal symptoms, or it would remind the addict that they have the "wrong" addiction. On the other hand, when the addict is using—and is most likely happy, even for a short period of time—discussing the addiction could remind the user that they are, in fact, a user, thus making their happy emotions turn sour and become an unpleasant experience.

Remember: Addicts are volatile, and anyone living in that environment constantly will soon develop instincts based on that volatility. Which is why codependents and narcissists are not usually able to handle pressure, changing environments, or stress.

The second rule is to not trust. This one is pretty easy when we take the extreme form of addiction or abuse into context. Most addicts, once they get to the extreme stages, will use anything and everything to get money for their next fix. Including selling or using their children. Unfortunately, children pick up on these types of habits or tendencies pretty quickly, which will cause them to become incredibly distrustful of people in authority. Part of this is because their parents have wronged them, and another small bit will be based on the fact that no other adult in their circle—at least in their minds—has picked up on what is happening and done anything to help them. Sadly, this type of scenario is a lose-lose situation, where no matter what or how an adult behaves, there will be some flaw resulting in the child creating an inability to completely trust.

The third rule is to not feel. Again, when played out throughout the assumption that children would have experienced this type of abuse for long periods of time, it makes sense. After experiencing multiple yo-yo emotional scenarios, being lied to, lived through false-hope one too many times, the child will teach themselves to not feel anything. Most often they will use the lie that "it is better this way." And they are not entirely wrong. When there are no trustworthy adults, safe environments, or even a steady and constant environment for the child to learn and understand their vulnerabilities and how to navigate that in this world (which is hard even on its own), closing off their emotions is the "next best" choice of action.

In reality, it is not, but this type of logic does unfortunately make sense.

When it comes to abuse, most children or victims do not want to talk about it because it is embarrassing. Even children feel a sense of helpless embarrassment when they are abused, and may even convince themselves they deserved it somehow. They will not trust because they have either reached out to an authority figure before, and nothing was done, or they are unsure that any type of power would be able to stop the abuse and keep them safe. Children of abuse make sure that they do not feel so as to limit the types of hurt they experience, similar to the amnesia section (Peterson, 2018).

The Beginning of Healing

While both codependents and narcissists are created through a background of abuse or addiction each type of person handles this abuse differently, hence why there are two potential outcomes of people.

Since there are two types of people, this also means that there are different healing processes as well; and then that healing process needs to be further divided into an understanding that it will need to be individualized for each person and their specific trauma.

What you need to understand is that everyone has their own healing process, and while generalized steps are a good way to begin thinking about how to start healing, there may be more required steps per individual.

Journaling

This chapter was a lot to go through, so first: take a few deep breaths. Make yourself a cup of tea or coffee if you need to, but be sure to come back and really think about what you have read.

Now that you have taken a moment, ask yourself: have you experienced any of these things within yourself or your partner? If so, what were they? Explicitly write down the situation, scenario, and trigger, along with your own feelings from that moment and now, after reading the chapter and as you are reliving that experience in a safe place.

CHAPTER 3

The Tangled Love Story

Ever heard of the saying, "opposites attract," or perhaps something that might be less familiar, "we marry our parents"?

Well, this may or may not be true all the time, it is definitely a little bit more common for codependent and narcissistic/addictive relationships. Part of this is because, on the surface, the two are "complimentary": One thrives off of the attention given by others, and the other lives to serve (Villines, 2018). It may be true that this type of arrangement works for a while, but eventually, things will start to get messy.

When a codependent or narcissist gets into a relationship and becomes too comfortable, they will intrinsically begin to create a more chaotic environment, since that will mimic what they are comfortable in through extended exposure (this is not just true for these types of people or relationship, however). Now, before jumping off your couch and going "That isn't comfortable when I'm in it!": That is exactly the point.

Due to their childhood/background of addiction and chaos, the brains and emotional understanding of narcissistic and codependent people have become skewed to believe that an unhealthy and disruptive environment is what they are comfortable in. In reality, they are just very good at surviving it, and even then, there will be a time limit.

The problem then becomes how to understand when you, or someone you know, is letting their background of addiction, coupled with their codependent or narcissistic tendencies, ruin what might be a good thing, or sabotage something that could have been saved. This is exactly what we will explore in this chapter, through both sides of the coin. Then, we will discuss how to begin untangling and recognizing where certain patterns and behaviors are coming into play in upcoming chapters.

Codependents

When it comes to romantic relationships, codependents will seek partners who will continue the patterns of dysfunction they were raised in; and this habit will either be conscious or unconscious. Thanks to the type of environments a codependent attachment type will crave, they will likely continue to get into relationships with: addicts, manipulators, abusers, or emotionally unavailable people. While they may not be the pick of the bunch for some, to a codependent, these types of people are everything they could ever want and more.

Why?

Because each of these types of people will give a codependent person something to work with. Each person, in their own way, will present unique challenges and problems that a codependent will be able to sink into to begin helping and fixing the person to be better. The problem is that often, these types of people are not willing to be fixed or become better. What codependents often do not want to hear, is that change has to happen in the person who needs to change through the manifestation, acknowledgement, and follow-through of a want.

It could be any want, such as: wanting a better job, wanting to be sober, wanting to fulfill their potential. Anyone can change, but only when the person who needs to change is willing to put in the work. Which ultimately leaves anyone who is "along" on this journey on the sidelines and unable to be anything other than support in times of need and encouragement. This type of arrangement will work perfectly well with someone who understands boundaries and has a healthy acceptance of themselves and their wants and needs. But to a codependent this is the absolute worst arrangement imaginable. Because codependents thrive on giving beyond what is appropriate, reasonable, or honest, in a relationship.

In comparison, people who are: addicts, manipulators, abusers, or emotionally unavailable and have absolutely no desire to change, will find a codependents desire to go above and beyond what is a good idea, incredibly appealing and desirable.

Or, look at it this way: a codependent will give beyond what is necessary or appropriate for a relationship, whereas a narcissist will take an inappropriate amount of whatever is being offered, by their significant other.

But that is not the only way a codependent can act in a relationship. They can also be controlling, insecure people pleasers who will control their partners while trying to constantly please them, creating an intoxicating mix of acting like their own needs and wants are not important. And it will definitely seem that way; which is by no means a green flag to go and do that. What it does mean is that you need to be careful and be aware of when certain things begin to be controlled by a codependent, or when their partner has taken too much of the center stage in their lives.

Compared to narcissists, who are demanding and selfish, codependents will appear to be more passive and giving, and on the one hand: they will be. To the point where their own identity and needs will not matter.

Which also leads into another identifier: Codependents will be too entangled in the emotions of their partner, along with their own reactions and subsequent triggers, to create a healthy communicating relationship. Sooner or later, shame-based actions and communications will begin to take place. Examples of phrases that are shame-based are:

- "Do not talk about that."

- "It is your fault that happened."

- "Do not feel."

- "It is your job to protect me and keep me happy."

- "My bad."

On the one hand, to some people these phrases may seem innocuous if a bit too absolutist. Yet underneath, you can begin to see that these phrases are controlling, refusing to accept blame for their share of an event or mistake, as well as completely ignoring that they have any clout or responsibility in the relationship.

Eventually, codependents will actually become incredibly confused over the situation they have created. They will be completely unaware of their part in creating any feelings of negativity, hostility, the re-introduction of a chaotic environment, the people pleasing, or the controlling behaviors. Nevertheless, with the introduction of any and all of these things, a codependent person will begin to react to this type of environment by regressing back into their inner-child response, which in turn, will cause them to become insecure and incredibly angry at the situation.

Sounds like a lot, and a little impossible, right? Well, let's break it down further.

The Love Triangle

It may seem odd, but codependents love live triangles. Specifically one that involves: them, their partner, and something else, like an addiction (but normally not a person). Again, part of this is because a codependent person will either consciously, or unconsciously, pick someone who will ensure that their 'comfortable' emotional space from their childhood/background, will eventually become present (i.e., addiction, or abuse/neglect).

To a codependent person, it may feel like a string of bad luck, or they could even convince themselves that they are not the reason all of their past significant others were addicts, or became addicts over time. It is incredibly uncomfortable to acknowledge, but when there becomes a list that is considerably long, and every single one of those people in that list are an addict or have something wrong with them, the only common denominator is: you/the other person.

This principle is something that codependent people will never fully understand; because they believe that their willingness to help, and intrinsic need to fix another person, will be so good it would be impossible for that to cause someone to go "bad." Unfortunately, they are very wrong.

How Easy They Fall

All it takes is one experience to be hooked on codependency in childhood, adolescence or early adulthood. This happens because it develops through a long-term relationship with an unstable, needy, or even mentally ill person. This could include someone who is an addict, overly protective, domineering, and/or highly controlling.

When we are young, that is when most of our habits, thoughts, and patterns begin to develop. That is not to say that they cannot be broken, they can. But when they are formed at such a young and impressionable age, breaking these habits and instinctive behaviors is harder, and takes years of intensive therapy to begin breaking down and understanding them.

Another way that codependency is created in young children through relationships is by learning the behavior through watching or experiencing. Yes, all codependents are "created," for lack of a better term, through childhood trauma experienced due to addiction and some form of abuse. However, this type of scenario is also a front row seat to watching codependent behavior (remember how opposites attract?) and how to handle these types of situations as a codependent. When a child of abuse is uncertain of their identity, and then one that appears to kind of work is presented, it is pretty hard to not use that as a model for yourself (yes, that sounds incredibly off-putting, but it is true).

And then comes the actual fall of a codependent: as mentioned in the introduction of this chapter, anyone who has had a troubling, abusive, chaotic, or essentially traumatic childhood, will begin to intrinsically create chaos and sabotaging patterns of behavior if they are unaware of their actions. When it comes to codependents, this type of behavior generally comes out as controlling. On the one hand, this sounds a little odd, since so far, codependents have been viewed as the "easy-going" ones in comparison to narcissists. However, remember that codependents need you to need them while simultaneously being the savior of their partner. Meaning that when things are "too" good, or they are uncomfortable, they will begin to push and control things they believe they should be controlling— such as a partner's sobriety journey, work life, or even friends and activities—to "better" their partner (Villines, 2018). While this may go well at first, sooner or later tactics such as guilt, manipulation, or shame will be used to continue encouraging their partner in certain behaviors over time; and no one particularly enjoys those types of ploys.

Narcissists

Compared to codependents, narcissists will actually prefer and look for a codependent, or someone who has a not-stable identity, as a partner. Again, part of this is because this is the type of relationship that they have seen "work" in their childhood, but another part of it is because they intrinsically know that this type of person will fulfill their innermost need: to be the best at the cost of someone else and have their needs always be put first (Kassel, 2022).

How It Starts

Now that you have a stronger idea of what narcissists are, it may seem surprising that you, or someone you know, actually got into a relationship with one. After all, they are slightly obvious to spot. Honestly, they are on paper or in comparison to codependents; but they are actually quite a bit harder to spot in person when you do not know them well.

Why? Because they begin any type of relationship with a lot of charm and setting up the ideal fantasy, which plays into their narcissistic personality disorder (NPD) (Kassel, 2022). Whether it is obvious or not, narcissists thrive off of fantasy. This fantasy could be anything from imagining their superior qualities (intellect, work ethic, abilities, etc.), to how good they can be as a partner; and that may actually happen for a little bit (Kassel, 2022). The problem is that overtime, their seemingly perfect qualities, like their: attentiveness, willingness to go the extra mile for you, presents, etc., will begin to fade (Kassel, 2022).

Practical Note

A great example of how this could happen is if someone comes on too strong, too soon. For instance, if they constantly point out how perfect you two are, how they complete you, or how you are their ideal partner and vice versa, you may want to start being careful (Kassel, 2022).

This does not mean that fairytales do not happen, or are concrete signs that the person you have just started to see is in fact a narcissist: but it does create a yellow flag that you should watch out for. Normally, in most adult (or relatively experienced) relationships if someone keeps pushing about how perfect they/the relationship are immediately—and you are still unsure (think of a pushy salesman who keeps trying to get you to purchase something you are really unsure of)—then take that as a sign of your subconscious telling you something might not be entirely right.

Another great note is if connections you had at the beginning actually begin to disappear. Things like: common hobbies, things you liked to talk about, or places you liked to go. Sure, relationships evolve and change over time, and people have a right to change their opinions. But the minute someone lies to even start a relationship, there is a problem.

True love grows over time. It begins through a spark or connection and then deepens through commonalities and affection for the other person. Love with a narcissist will be a hollow and fake simulation of that, until one day you forgot why you are even there in the first place.

The Love Triangle

When it comes to narcissists, they will often be the ones who are either the addict, or present very much like an addict in a relationship. Like addicts, narcissists will often present emotional volatility, will act withdrawn and moody when their way/"fix"/needs are not being met, present a lack of empathy towards anyone, including their partner, and make it incredibly hard for their significant others to leave through multiple manipulation tactics (Kassel, 2022).

Why this is classified as a love triangle is because often the significant other of a narcissist is in love with two very different people: the charming person who was originally portrayed at the beginning of the relationship—and perhaps when they recognize that their partner is about to leave and need them to stay—and the actual narcissist. Honestly, the narcissist is unaware this love triangle truly exists. To them, both parts are the same person. Sadly, they are not wrong: both the charming and the narcissistic side are the same person. The problem is that you—as the significant other—most likely fell in love with one, and ended up with the other. Hence the love triangle.

How It Goes

When it comes to narcissists, they do not traditionally "fall" until they get their moment of revelation that they are actually sucking the joy and personality out of their significant others, if that moment ever comes. Some narcissists can go their whole lives without realizing what they are. It will always be that the other person was not good enough, was the problem, or was no longer "caring and into saving the relationship." Like with any other person that lives in chosen ignorance; it is impossible for the loved ones of a narcissist to do anything until they want to change themselves.

Instead, partner's will experience everything from: gaslighting, refusal to apologize, lack of attention or empathy, and manipulation tactics to continue not giving their partner what they need, while still receiving everything they need and more. Remember: narcissists will take an inappropriate amount of whatever their partner offers, including: affection, attention, money, gifts, etc. It really does not matter; if it is offered, they will take it.

Yes, this sounds incredibly depressing and like a bad place to be: And it is. There is no sugarcoating it. Dating or being in close contact consistently with a narcissist is draining. You may not notice it immediately, but over time it will become incredibly obvious, if not to you, it will to those around you.

Do Not Forget the Chaos

When it comes to creating chaos in a relationship to continue their own sense of comfort: a narcissist will do that intrinsically on their own, to meet their own needs. Where codependents will often do it to create an environment they are comfortable in, narcissists will begin to create chaos because they need more from the relationship.

This chaos could come in the forms that were previously mentioned such as: gaslighting, manipulation, lack of empathy, and refusal to apologize for their inappropriate behavior. The word 'chaos' might seem too strong for this type of situation, but for those living in it; it is a pretty good description. Going from a caring, perhaps almost too loving and attentive partner, to a distant, needy, and manipulative one within a short span of time is chaotic and confusing to someone who is not aware of what is going on around them.

CHAPTER 4

Happiness, Peace, and Joy Are Out of Reach

You may very well be in a place where you feel like happiness, peace, and joy are out of reach. Whether that is because you have not yet forgiven yourself, are unable to move forward, or perhaps because you are still unsure if you are in a relationship with a narcissistic or codependent person. First of all, know that having these feelings or thoughts are completely valid. There are times when all of us are so lost in our current emotions and circumstances that it is impossible to think that we are ever going to get out.

But know this: you can get out of it. Regardless of the reason, it is entirely possible for you to become happy, peaceful, and joyous on a regular basis again. But it will take some work for you to get there.

The turning point in any type of relationship which requires change is understanding that *you* have to change. Yes, your partner/the other person most likely has to as well, but this book is geared towards helping you change. Hopefully, by now, you are starting to connect the dots between certain habits and/or problems that keep popping up in your life, and some of the changes that have been recommended or hinted at so far. Now it is time for us to begin moving onto the intermediary step: discovering and re-framing your negative thought patterns.

A Few Notes

Before diving into how you can actually get happiness, joy, and peace in your life there are a few things to discuss.

First of all, some of you may have been reading along hoping that a magical elixir on how to fix your current—and most likely toxic—relationship would come up. Sadly, that is not the case. If you have not caught on yet, it is time for this chapter to hit you with the biggest and hardest struggle with any codependent or narcissistic, or any, relationship: if they do not want to change, they will not. You, however, do. Or at least, it is assumed that you do, since you are reading this book.

This juxtaposition means two things: first, you can change. Because you want to. If you want to, you can do it. With the help of a good support community and knowledge, anything is possible. Second, just because your partner does not want to change does not mean that anything is wrong with you, that you are unworthy, or that your relationship was always wrong/bad. It simply means that they do not want to. That is it, that is all.

It sucks, it hurts, and it is never something anyone wants to hear. But there you have it.

If this is you, do not let your partner's unwillingness to change condemn you both to a life of half-moments of happiness, peace, or joy. You deserve more than that.

Second, relationships only change and evolve when both of you put in the work. If you are willing, but the other person is not, then the relationship will ultimately not change. Sure, little things may happen, but over time the big life-altering types of changes you intrinsically want, will never come to be. So you have to begin to think about what you really want; along with what you actually deserve.

Third, you are not responsible for making someone else want to change and be better. We would all love it if when our partner hears us asking them to change, they would; and some do. But that is not everyone's story, personality, or ability. And we—as the other person—have to be okay with that. Just as you are fighting to gain your independence through boundaries and self-identity, so too, do you have to let them have theirs.

Fourth, this chapter is going to really drive home (before even beginning to discuss boundaries) that in order to feel happiness, peace, and joy, you are going to have to be willing and comfortable dealing and providing these emotions for yourself, by yourself. That does not mean a partner cannot come along and help; but if you make it all up to your partner, you are asking for an unfair and unhealthy exchange of relational duties.

Fifth, this chapter marks a switch that is going to happen within this book. We are now 'done' individualizing and explaining codependents and narcissists in general. Now it is time to focus on you, how to stand tall, how to be on your own, and how to heal from those relationships. What this also means is that you may experience moments where you are going to experience a lot of inner struggles.

This could be because you are not ready to read what is in here, or that you are unwilling to accept some of the hard truths which are going to be brought into actuality. Whatever the reason; taking a deep breath to think and really see if this is what you are struggling with/should do, is never a harmful thing to do when you are overwhelmed. Take as long as you need. Additionally, you are going to begin fighting a lot of personal demons from this chapter onwards. Do not let this become an opportunity to beat yourself up. Instead, use it as a learning experience. Note areas/days/times/situations/concepts where you are maybe lacking or not as strong, and use those chapters and helpful notes to begin figuring out how you can get better and stronger for upcoming relationships and scenarios.

Intrinsically, use this chapter—and the rest—to focus on yourself and your healing.

That was a lot of heavy-hitting notes for a chapter dealing with happiness, peace, and joy. But all of them were needed immediately in this chapter because from here on out, we are dealing specifically with you. Which is why we have to get some of the lies you may have been telling yourself, or maybe even the fears that were starting to surface, out of the way.

Now, onto the actual chapter.

Negative Thinking

It may seem a bit over-simplistic to state, or even discuss, but negative thinking is one of the top reasons anyone has a hard time reaching happiness, peace, joy, or even a sense of calmness, throughout their day, let alone in their lives. Negative thinking is sometimes blamed too arbitrarily for certain things we tend to do regularly, such as when we do not set ourselves up for success, or actually follow-through certain scenarios and then end up having problems. But on the other hand, the true problem with negative thinking is perhaps never fully appreciated by many people.

However, if you come from a place of addiction—even as a

background—negative thinking may be more ingrained in your mental patterns than you know. That is not to say that negative thinking cannot be ingrained in someone who does not come from those backgrounds; however, the cycle of addiction has a lot of negativity and self-hatred associated/built into it, so there is a higher correlation between the two. In fact, most often, when an addict relapses, negative thinking about the relapse has started days or weeks before the actual event (Hammers-Crowell, 2019).

You may be wondering how any of that applies to you. Well, ever have this nagging little voice in your head that your negative self-talk, thinking, perspective, or even anticipation is what is making your life worse?

Here is the truth for you: It is.

Sad, hurtful, maybe even hard to acknowledge or accept, but it is.

What Is It?

First, before going into how negativity is getting in your way, a lot of which is due to the trauma you have experienced in your narcissistic, codependent, or addictive relationships, we should probably have a firm idea of what it is first.

It may sound overly simplistic for the harm it causes, but negative thinking is really just constantly thinking in the negative

(Better Help Editorial Team, 2022a). This goes beyond recognizing where things could go wrong, or being realistic about certain outcomes due to the input in certain situations or various other factors. For instance, if you know that you have not done the best of jobs studying for an exam, saying, "I might have failed that exam," is not negative thinking.

Negative thinking is when you constantly pick the most negative and worse outcome possible and literally only allow that outcome to exist in your mental play-by-play of that scenario. This includes: criticizing yourself, expecting the worst outcome, or expecting the people around you to constantly disappoint you. So for the exam example, this would look like studying all night and actually doing a good job, but still saying that you most likely failed.

Yes, some of you may very well have lived a life where that is expected, and it is most likely very unhelpful to simply say, "Stop," or, "That may not always happen." This is not what this chapter is advocating, by any means. What it is trying to do is point out how often you actually set yourself up—maybe even subconsciously—to expect the negative and encourage that type of outcome along.

Negativity Is Making It Worse

Which brings up the real question of: how could this be making it worse? Well, for starters, any type of negative thinking exacerbates narcissistic or codependent mentalities, especially through the cycle of addiction. In addicts, negativity is one of the key reasons they can experience a relapse (Hammers-Crowell, 2019). Generally how this works is through three stages: emotional, mental, and physical. During the emotional stage, the actual emotions of an addict begin to set them up for relapsing. This could be seen in not being as careful on how they handle their daily mental monologues, or making sure that their habits are completely opposite/not associated with old user habits. This primes users for the mental stage, which is where the user begins to think about their old vice of choice, and how their current circumstances justify re-introducing that vice back into their daily lives. Which then brings us to the physical stage: where addicts actually do break down and re-introduce their addictive substance, or maybe another just as addictive substance, into their lives (Hammers-Crowell, 2019).

When we look at this particular cycle, it becomes pretty obvious how the negative thinking jump started the relapse: It was because they were not guarding their thoughts and emotions to ensure that they validated their negative feelings, without prolonging or worsening them beyond the actual scope of what was happening.

So, then, let's take this concept and transfer it onto codependents, narcissists, or those who have been in a relationship with them. A relationship with a mentally unhealthy person is going to create an unhealthy relationship if that person is not in intensive therapy or taking care of themselves. As shown in previous chapters, codependent and narcissistic relationships, in particular, mimic abusive and addictive relationships through exhibited behaviors and mindsets. Meaning that negative thinking will be just as prevalent in these types of relationships as addictive ones. Codependent and narcissistic relationships will experience how negative thinking causes relapses in behaviors or promised changes, along with continued increased negative thinking within the partners of these relationships.

Understanding that your partner could experience a relapse is something most people who get romantically involved with an addict should be aware of. Yet when it comes to a codependent or narcissist, relapse is not a word that is generally used, but it should be. Just like an addict, codependents and narcissists are capable of changing (if they want to), and just like an addict, they can become a healthy and not toxic person to be with in a relationship. However, the road to get there is long and filled with many side-journeys and re-visits of old behaviors and concepts. Which brings us full circle to the concept of "relapses" in these types of relationships. For a codependent or narcissist a relapse may not actually be an addictive substance; it may be something worse, such as old behaviors or mind games.

Think about it: A codependent needs you to need them, and a

narcissist needs you to make them everything. Both of these concepts are a lack of self-identity, but these lacks of self-identity are gained through manipulation and mind-games on their partners, so that they get what they want and are still able to appear like they are caring, loving, and supportive of their partner (there may be a few areas where they actually are; some codependents and narcissists do not express this behavior over every aspect of life). To them, these mind-games are their bread and butter. It is how they get what they want, it is how they keep you happy, and it is how they maintain and keep their identity. None of which is healthy and all of which, mimics the relationship between an addict and an enabler.

The only difference is how the "relapse" appears in the relationship. In an addictive relationship the relapse often appears in the form of an addictive substance. In a codependent or narcissistic relationship this relapse will appear through the re-introduction of mind games that the partner has promised to not do anymore in the hopes of having a healthier relationship. These behaviors could be things such as: manipulation, guilt-tripping, lack of empathy, or inability to share the spotlight/attention with their partner.

For someone who has dealt with a codependent or narcissistic relationship and its toxic results, a relapse in any or all of them, is not a pleasant occurrence.

How Is It Worse?

A valid question some people might be having is: how does the knowledge of negative thinking make any of this worse? From the sounds of it a relationship with a codependent or narcissistic person was already an unhappy and unhealthy one, so how could it get worse?

Well, simple: being aware of negative thinking helps you notice what you are reacting to, rather than responding to. In any type of relationship the difference between reacting and responding is a big one. When we react to things, we often do not think or mentally edit as we say or act: Whatever happens, happens, but it never stays in that moment. Often, the things we say when we are reacting, come out repeatedly in different fights/scenarios. Even healthy relationships can have month-long after-affects from a poor reaction. This could be something like throwing an old flame in your significant other's face, or pointing out a past fight that was supposedly forgiven, but obviously has not been.

In comparison, a response is when you have the time and ability to think, filter, and then give an answer/corresponding action. Being able to take that split-second to think and filter can save any relationship tons of agony and grief.

Add on top of that, being aware of negative thinking and you suddenly have the magical elixir to potentially saving a relationship you were maybe hoping for (again, this is really being written in extreme hesitation, because your partner has to want to change and work on being healthy together).

Think about it: being aware of your negative thinking patterns and triggers will help you gain another way to notice when you are reacting or responding. And you being aware and willfully choosing if you are going to react or respond, will give you the ability to begin choosing to respond in ways that could be beneficial and saving to your current, or future, relationship.

Build the Awareness

Now that you know what negativity is and how it is making things worse, it is time for you to begin considering how to build your awareness of your negative thinking patterns.

Practice Mindfulness and Self-Awareness

Making sure that you are consciously present and being mindful of what you allow your brain to think at any moment is key in building your awareness of how and when your negative thinking comes into play (Cuncic, 2020). It will help you begin to gain an almost out-of-body mindfulness, which you can use to help your response/react ratio.

Identify Them

Once you are able to be mindful and self-aware, you need to begin recognizing which types of negative thinking you utilize. It could be multiple types and depend on certain scenarios and triggers. Or, it could be one predominant type. Either way, knowing which type you tend to gravitate towards will help you begin to create a formula on how to combat and identify your negative thoughts. There are multiple types of negative thoughts such as: jumping to conclusions, catastrophizing (making everything to be the worst possible outcome), over generalizing, labeling, using "should" emotions to make yourself feel guilty and inadequate, using your emotions as the base "truth" of a scenario, and personalization and blaming (Cuncic, 2020).

Replacements

Replacing negative thoughts is tricky, and is something we will discuss more in depth in the upcoming chapter. So for now, begin to note and acknowledge that you are not being asked to only recognize and identify the types of negative thinking you experience and then that is all that will be said on the topic. You will be given tools and examples on how to replace your negative thoughts; because your brain simply cannot stop something. It will need a replacement activity.

A Few Notes

Which brings us up to a few things that should be mentioned before continuing. First of all: Making yourself stop negative thinking by ignoring those thoughts/emotions, or essentially not allowing yourself to be negative at all, is the exact opposite of what actually stopping negative thinking looks like. Stopping your brain from even acknowledging that certain emotions exist is unhealthy and a good way to build even more negative thought patterns and habits around those specific scenarios or triggers. While it may seem easier to do in the beginning, undoing those particular actions and habits are harder to break and longer to become consistent in.

Really consider using your journal to help you begin coping with negative thoughts. Specifically, to help you notice your patterns, the types you use, and what triggers you in each specific scenario. It is amazing how returning to those entries hours or days later—long enough to have gained some objectivity—can help you see patterns or problems more easily.

CHAPTER 5

The Process of Achieving Interdependence

Whether you are fighting codependency, narcissism, or know someone with either of these things, achieving interdependence is possible. You may find yourself in a different stage/place in life when this journey is over—and that is okay—but it is not the intention of this book to encourage you to leave current relationships for newer and better things. On the other hand, it does not *not* encourage you to leave, either.

Small Note

However, that does not include abuse, of any kind. If, throughout any part of reading this book or talking to friends, family, a counselor and/or therapist, you feel like you are in an unsafe and unhealthy relationship: reach out to someone who is safe for you, to begin making an exit strategy.

Even if you are in a relationship with a codependent or

narcissistic person, it does not mean you have, or should, stay if there is abuse, addiction, or extremely dangerous behaviors or habits around you. That is nowhere near what this book is encouraging.

So, with that out of the way, let's begin to discuss cognitive behavioral therapy and how it can be used to help you achieve interdependence.

What Is It?

Cognitive behavioral therapy (CBT) is a type of therapy that can be used either on individuals or couples, depending on preferences and needs. The goal of CBT is to help practitioners achieve a solution-based way of overcoming problems they are encountering in their mental health. Couples who use CBT also notice additional benefits such as: improved communication, a higher practice of rewarding relational behaviors, and the awareness and ability to reevaluate harmful assumptions made by either person which are harming the relationship as a whole.

CBT works to combine your thoughts, feelings, and behaviors to help you feel better and function more proactively and healthily in situations you may find difficult (Cognitive Behavioral Therapy Los Angeles, n.d.). Compared to other types of therapy, CBT is goal-orientated, meaning that it will target certain behaviors and feelings to help you achieve a specific goal. This could be anything from finding a job to achieving healthier and better relationships with others. Due to its relatively open-ended approach, CBT can be used in any type of relationship, including: romantic, friendship, or familial. Making it a perfect option for those dealing with codependent or narcissistic relationships; however they look.

How It Works

CBT is goal-orientated, meaning that the therapist and the patient have to work in tandem to identify problems and associated triggers, along with brainstorming, choosing, and practicing practical solutions in those situations. Because CBT is a highly active and response-based therapy, practitioners have to be careful to ensure mindfulness and consistency when working and using the solutions they have decided on with their therapist.

Normally these actions include self-help assignments such as thought journals and specific CBT tools, assigned by the therapist, to help patients be proactive in their mental health journey, instead of only being reactive and responsive when difficult situations come up (Cognitive Behavioral Therapy Los Angeles, n.d.). A great example of these tools would be cognitive restructuring. Cognitive restructuring is the process of helping people change the way they think. For instance, if someone is stressed in a situation, cognitive restructuring would encourage that person to replace the stressful thoughts with more balanced thoughts, to help reduce stress in that moment, or to do the same with negative thinking (University of Concordia Health Services, n.d.). Using CBT to help introduce and consistently use cognitive restructuring can help patients begin to change their negative thought patterns (remember the last chapter?) into more helpful and adaptive responses to produce a better outcome (Cognitive Behavioral Therapy Los Angeles, n.d.). By identifying, challenging, and replacing intrusive and unhelpful thoughts with objective, and more realistic thoughts, CBT is able to help overcome years of built-in response techniques within a person's brain in a short span of time.

A few other techniques and approaches that therapists who use CBT can introduce to help address particular thoughts, emotions, and behaviors, include: journaling, role-playing, relaxation techniques, and mental distractions (Cognitive Behavioral Therapy Los Angeles, n.d.).

Since CBT is incredibly personalized to the patient, their mental health, their specific problems and associated triggers, along with their personalized reactions, it is really hard to give generalized specifics aside from what has already been discussed. However, because this type of treatment is so "broad" in explanation, but so specific in treatment, the beauty and simplicity of this combination cannot be undermined in patients who decide to use this type of therapy.

Who Uses It?

Anyone can use CBT, and to a lot of people it is incredibly appealing since it is meant to achieve results within a short time-span while additionally tackling pre-existing mental reactions and conditions. But there are just as many other specific types of therapeutic approaches which involve CBT. Because CBT focuses on identifying and changing negative and distorted thought patterns, emotional responses, and behaviors, it can be used in multiple approaches, including:

- Dialectical behavior therapy (DBT) addresses thoughts and behaviors while incorporating strategies such as emotional regulations and mindfulness. When using this approach, introducing, or using aspects of CBT are already not that far behind (Cognitive Behavioral Therapy Los Angeles, n.d.).

- Multimodal therapy suggests that psychological issues must be treated by addressing seven different but interconnected modalities, specifically: behavior, affect, sensation, imagery, cognition, interpersonal factors, and drug/biological considerations. Using CBT to help therapists and patients combat their behaviors, affects, and parts of the cognition, would help move that particular therapeutic approach along (Cognitive Behavioral Therapy Los Angeles, n.d.).

- Rational emotive behavior therapy (REBT) involves identifying irrational beliefs, actively challenging them, and beginning to recognize and change those patterns (Cognitive Behavioral Therapy Los Angeles, n.d.).

Notice how all three of these examples of therapeutic approaches could, and do, involve aspects of CBT? It is amazing how much our behaviors and responses are linked to everything else that we perceive to be wrong with us. It is even more interesting to see how the minute we focus on healing those particular parts of ourselves, we are able to reach out and attain certain forms of mental health we never previously thought possible.

Benefits of CBT

There are many benefits to CBT, a lot of which have already been discussed, but let's just put them all down into a list to help visualize why it might be a good consideration for you (Mayo Clinic, 2019) (Cognitive Behavioral Therapy Los Angeles, n.d.):

- A strong feeling of personalized inclusion and responsibility with your own mental health

- A stronger and better understanding of your own responsibilities in a relationship

- Better ways to communicate with others and to help navigate tricky discussions to get resolutions

- Creating better mental neural pathways in stressful and bad situations to achieve better outcomes

- Not relying on drugs for your mental health

- Creating adaptable plans for future problems that you may be unaware of

- A stronger sense of self-awareness and mindfulness

- Better skills for coping with: grief, loss, miscommunication, stress, criticism, or anger

- Able to identify and manage your emotions

Potential Challenges

As with all types of therapy or solutions, there are challenges with cognitive behavioral therapy; and just as with all of the benefits, you should be aware of some of the challenges you may face if you decide to use it.

First of all, change is difficult, and a big part of introducing and using CBT methods, is to change parts of your behaviors. Pay attention to this: CBT is going to encourage you to change your behaviors and thoughts, but it does not mean changing you as a human. Your likes, dislikes, personality, goals, and dreams should remain relatively the same. And that will not be particularly easy; there will be days where that change will be hard to do—it may even feel impossible—but it is worth it.

Second, introducing and using CBT is incredibly structured. Meaning that it is often better suited to clients who are more comfortable in a structured and focused environment. Part of this is because to introduce and use CBT, a therapist will become a therapist and instructor within one session; and some people are not always comfortable, or able, to have someone be two roles at once within that short time period.

Third, due to its structure and focus, CBT does not tend to focus on underlying unconscious resistances to change which you may have built up over time. Other approaches, such as psychoanalytic psychotherapy, however, do focus on the subconscious and underlying problems. This does not mean that CBT would be a bad fit for you, but you should be aware that it will only go so far. If you are looking for something which will go that in-depth, you may have to start off with CBT and then graduate onto something more later on.

Fourth, you have to be willing to change. It has been said multiple times in this book, and it will be said again. Nothing will happen if you are not willing to actually change. This includes embracing the uncomfortable, the things you do not like, and admitting where you may be wrong. This situation is most likely not entirely your fault, but completely dodging the blame for your actions will also get you nowhere. Especially with CBT. Because CBT is focusing on your behaviors, thoughts, actions, and the relationship between all three; if you are unwilling or unable to own up and try to begin recognizing where you went wrong and how, then you may not get the most out of this type of therapy. Or this book, for that matter.

Fifth, is that for all the hullabaloo about this type of therapy being goal-oriented, it will still be gradual. Change doesn't happen overnight. It happens with consistency, and sadly, consistency takes time. The reason consistency takes time is because you have to build up the mental stamina and habit to actually begin making that change your go-to action, rather than the years of built-up response actions you have been using so far. So, if you notice that it is taking a while, do not lose heart. You are on the right path, it will just take longer than expected.

So What?

While parts of this chapter may have begun to read like a scientific journal, rather than a self-help book, it is necessary for you to understand the types of therapy that are available to you while on this journey. Blindly trusting and going into any type of scenario that seems 'remotely helpful' is a good way to get into bad therapy and potentially make the trauma and damage you are trying to heal and get rid of worse.

Understanding and knowing how CBT is used is important so that when you reach out for professional help, you will already be familiar with some of these tactics. Honestly, you may just look it up online and try to do it yourself (while this is not really recommended, no one is stopping you from doing that either). And in either scenario it is better to be prepared with terminology and practices.

Back at It

So, going back to CBT and how it can be used in your particular relationship, let's begin to take a closer look.

In Relationships

Because CBT is goal-orientated, it allows therapists and patients to focus on specific problems/instances immediately; including relational problems such as communication. Additionally, CBT works hard to help couples who use it to reevaluate harmful assumptions which may be driving a wedge between partners, as well as increase rewarding and impactful behaviors within the relationship (Cognitive Behavioral Therapy Los Angeles, n.d.). This includes recognizing troubling behaviors in a relationship and accepting other types of behaviors that have been causing problems in the relationship (Cognitive Behavioral Therapy Los Angeles, n.d.). However, CBT does not encourage abusive, problematic, manipulative, or dishonest behaviors. So, the sentence saying "accepting other types of behaviors" never includes anything that would be putting someone into a dangerous, harmful, or distressing situation.

Other behaviors, however, such as leaving socks on the floor can cause a disproportionate number of problems in some relationships, and if there is already a pattern of miscommunication and an inability to understand one another in the heat of the moment—with no post-argument resolution tactics—CBT is where couples can find help. By focusing on acceptance and change management strategies, CBT enables couples to see past little discrepancies or miscommunication tactics, to create a healthy and thriving relationship (Cognitive Behavioral Therapy Los Angeles, n.d.).

While the above scenario could in fact include familial

relationships, CBT goes one step further when applied towards those connections. Specifically, the therapist and therapy plans begin to look at family dynamics between members, as well as how each of those members may or may not be contributing to functional and dysfunctional behaviors (Cognitive Behavioral Therapy Los Angeles, n.d.). Because family relationships often include more than two people, it is important for the therapist and the family to understand how each particular person is responsible in a certain situation.

With Codependents and Narcissists

Alright, now all that happy and encouraging talk about CBT probably has some of you wondering how it relates to achieving interdependence after a relationship with a codependent or narcissistic person; or maybe even in that relationship.

What Interdependence Is

First, let's discuss interdependence in a relationship. Interdependence is being able to appreciate your romantic relationship while still fully acknowledging and maintaining a strong sense of self and a self-identity (Clarke, 2021). As we have now thoroughly discussed, this type of strong sense of self *and* being able to identify as someone happily in a relationship is something that is not possible for people who are either with or are, a codependent or narcissistic person. Generally, a codependent or narcissistic person will ensure that they, or their partners, become dependent on them (or vice versa) within the relationship. Which goes against the concept of an interdependent relationship.

What It Looks Like

Honestly, even without being a codependent or narcissistic person—or being their partner—it is easy to see how being interdependent in a relationship is hard. Healthy, interdependent relationships understand that as a partner, you/they cannot be responsible for every aspect of the other person's life, and that expectation is non-existent (Clarke, 2021). This also means that partners do not find their worth in each other, or necessarily their relationship. Additionally, each person in an interdependent relationship works hard to meet their partner's emotional needs through meaningful ways, meaning that they actually learn about their partner and how to care for them in ways that are not compromising on either side (Clarke, 2021). But perhaps the scariest aspect of an interdependent relationship is that each person is able to let their partner get their sense of self from things outside of the relationship, such as: unshared hobbies, other friends, their family, etc. (Clarke, 2021).

According to Jodi Clarke from *VeryWellMind* here are a few other benefits of an interdependent relationship (Clarke, 2021):

- Healthy boundaries

- Active listening

- Time for personal interests

- Clear communication

- Taking personal responsibility for behaviors

- Creating a safe space so that each of you can be vulnerable

- Engaging and responding to each other

- Healthy self-esteem

- Being open and approachable with each other

Now, compared to a narcissistic person, it can become obvious pretty quickly when the relationship is not actually interdependent. But what about when you are comparing it to a codependent person?

Interdependent vs. Codependent

Part of the reason some people can confuse an interdependent relationship with a codependent one is because codependents may let someone believe they are in an interdependent relationship. On the surface, and certainly at the beginning, certain parts of the relationship will seem the same. Such as ensuring that your needs are met, that you are listened to, and that you are in a safe space. It is not until later in the relationship that those traits of a codependent relationship become hollow and ungenuine.

Here are a few examples on how codependency varies from interdependence:

- o Codependency

  - Puts others' needs before theirs all the time

  - Offers/provides help out of fear of abandonment, rejection and disapproval

  - Relies on praise from others for a sense of worth and self-esteem

  - Often has anxious attachment style

  - Poor personal boundaries

- o Interdependence

  - Pours into others after meeting their own needs first

  - Offers/provides help without guilt, resentment, fear, or anxiety

  - Practices regulation of their own emotions and are

willingly vulnerable

- Operates from secure attachment

- Has healthy boundaries

The good news is that with the help of CBT both codependents and narcissists are able to change—if they want to—and turn your relationship around. Or, if you are already no longer with that person, you can use CBT to help you gain a better sense of yourself and combat your traumas before going into the next relationship.

How to Start

There are a few practical ways to start preparing for cognitive behavioral therapy, if that is the way you decide to go.

First, do some research. Look into the certified therapists around you. Check their background and experience in cognitive behavioral therapy and look up to see reviews or comments from previous patients. You want to make sure not only that the therapist is right for you, but that their particular methods of CBT will be beneficial to your journey.

Second, prepare yourself. Take note of certain situations or areas you want control over and to better. It is always helpful to be proactive in these types of scenarios so that you can immediately delve right in and begin to look at your patterns and how to change them.

Chapter 6

Installing Strong Boundaries

Ah, boundaries. The long-awaited chapter (for some of you, at least). Even though boundaries are an intimidating thing to think about, once you are used to recognizing and respecting them, they become second nature. It will just take a lot of practice to get there.

First, just in case you have forgotten, a personal boundary is what you are, and are not, willing to accept in your personal and professional relationships. It really is as simple as that.

The problem with boundaries is that people often ignore, disrespect, or try to push or take on, their own, or other people's boundaries onto themselves or others.

For instance, at work your job is your job description. Yet so often jobs morph into other things. Sometimes it is because of job changes, managerial shifts, or company policy changes. Those are fine and acceptable shifts in a boundary. However, when a manager or boss expects more of you than you are paid for, or a team does none of the work but takes all of the credit, that is crossing a professional boundary. Whether or not you choose to point that out and do anything about it is up to you.

Our personal boundaries are always in place, you are just either unaware, or unwilling, to implement them. Again: It is what we know, acknowledge, and accept what we are, or are not, responsible for.

Narcissistic and Codependent Boundaries

The problem then, really becomes how narcissistic and codependent relationships obliterate all hope of personal boundaries, due to their lack of any. Think about it: the entire problem with narcissists or codependents is that they either put all their boundaries onto you, or take all of yours away in order to 'help' you. That may have seemed like an oversimplification, but in reality, it is not.

Let's walk that through for a moment.

Narcissist

When you are in a relationship with a narcissist, they do none of the work, but still want all of the glory associated with doing all of the work. Additionally, they will sacrifice their partner's happiness, comfort, and even peace of mind, to ensure that their reputation is spotless in all areas of life. Which is a really big lack of personal boundaries. Then, let's add on the biggest reason why a narcissist is the way they are: they lack a sense of self.

As seen in the previous chapter, a lack of sense of self is a good way to ensure that an interdependent relationship never happens; and boundaries are the cornerstone of that type of relationship.

Now, before going further we should point out that in some cases, narcissists are relatively unaware that they are actually stepping, or ignoring, your personal boundaries. Yes, there are those classic narcissists who know and do not care. But there are a very small percentage of them that are truly unaware of what they are doing (think of sociopaths and how they truly are not able to comprehend certain things, like empathy). This can happen to some narcissists.

Good news is that when you confront–and teach–that type of narcissist about their behavior, they may be willing to change; or at least consider it and try. Other narcissists on the other hand, the ones who know what they are doing, are a lost cause until they have a reason or incentive to change, which comes from outside of themselves.

With that little speech out of the way, let's take a look at how narcissists take away the personal boundaries of their partners.

Ethan (the narcissist) and Emily have been together for a little over a year. In the beginning, everything was great; the couple was happily in love. However, friends have begun to notice that Emily no longer corrected Ethan when he was wrong about her likes and dislikes, from food to fashion. Whatever Ethan wanted, Emily simply complied with. One time, when out with friends–and at the urging of the girlfriends in particular– Emily decided to confront Ethan about his ordering the wine for her (it was a wine she did not like and never had). When confronted, Ethan merely reminded Emily that she was wrong, and did she not remember previous dinners where she said she had liked it, and how well it paired with their meals? Did she suddenly no longer trust him?

In this example you see a great image of how narcissists use manipulation and gaslighting to ignore their partner's personal boundaries (yes, your likes and dislikes are a form of boundaries). After being confronted by Emily, Ethan ignored her clearly saying, "I do not like this," and instead reminded her of when she claimed to have liked it, and then turned it around into a ploy to ensure that he knew more than her, by asking if she no longer trusted his judgment.

The problem with narcissists and gaslighting is that it is slightly tricky in one-off situations, or "harmless" scenarios like this one. There are plenty of healthy relationships where partners forget that they previously liked something, or the other partner wonders why their knowledge is being questioned. However, in a healthy situation, neither of those actions are ever turned onto the other person in the form of a guilt/manipulation tactic.

Here, it was.

Ethan is a classic example of how a narcissist will ignore their partner's boundaries to infuse and grow their own ego and superiority in any circumstance.

Codependent

In comparison, codependents take away their own boundaries through the guise (now remember, they most likely are not doing it out of a sense of maliciousness) of helping.

On the one hand this almost seems like a dream come true. Someone who finally acknowledges all of your boundaries without any of the associated drama or necessary enforcing! But in reality, they are acknowledging your boundaries at the cost of their own, and while that might not be your fault, it is still not healthy. While it is nice when our boundaries are acknowledged and worked with, it is never good when they are the only ones in the relationship. Plus, since codependents create their value and sense of self off of their partner's—which will often dovetail into a partner's emotions—the lack of boundaries becomes an incredibly terrifying place to be for both parties.

Anytime someone sacrifices their own boundaries, even if they believe that is what they are meant to do in a relationship, they will not be happy. The problem for codependents is that they will often feel guilt for this anger and frustration, because they are generally not aware that denying their emotions is a red flag in the relationship. What is worse, is that the partner of a codependent is often unaware this is happening, so the eventual lash out of built up frustration from non-acknowledged boundaries will come as a confusing shock.

For instance:

Angela and Brad have been dating for about a year. However, over that time period, Brad's friends have been getting concerned. The once simple and lovely Angie has now become the ticking time-bomb of anger that none of Brad's friends can figure out. In their mind, her explosions and frustrated actions were disproportionate–and maybe even completely inappropriate and undeserved–to their friends' actions. What Brad's friends, and Brad, do not see is Angela's mental struggle every day with understanding why she is always so frustrated. So what if Brad does not do the dishes? Most partners do not. So what if he would rather play video games than cuddle with her (even though her rational mind knew he would if she asked)? Yet, inside, her frustration and internal anger would build at a terrifying level and eventually explode over a seemingly inconsequential action.

On the surface, it seems like Angela has a miscommunication problem; and she does. Most codependents suffer from multiple fears in relationships, including: the fear of rejection and confrontation. This means that many codependents will do whatever is easier, so that they can still be loved. Including not speaking up about their needs and wants in a relationship and stuffing their feelings so deep down, they can no longer distinguish where they came from.

In the above example, Angela knew her emotions and reactions were irrational, but she has not given herself the freedom to acknowledge that her personal boundaries of cleanliness and quality time were not being met by Brad in their relationship. Instead, she reasoned them away by acknowledging that he would do them if she asked; but she never asked.

How to Install Healthy Boundaries

Now that you have an idea on how boundaries might "exist" within a codependent or narcissistic relationship, but thanks to the examples provided know that those are not healthy boundaries, it is time to discuss how to actually begin creating and enforcing healthy boundaries within your life and relationships.

Recognize

Yourself

When it comes to you as a person, you need to recognize that for whatever reason, whether it be childhood trauma, previous relationships, or simple lack of awareness and teaching, somewhere along the line, you have created a life with no boundaries.

Not just that, you have created it to the point where you might not even be fully aware of it. You need to begin recognizing that.

Additionally, you need to sit down and think about which areas in your life could use boundaries. Often, people have strong and healthy-ish boundaries in one area, but have a complete lack of them in another. Building your self-awareness to understand where you need to focus on your boundaries (and this book will specifically cover relationships) is your first step.

As you build personal awareness remember: that just like other people in relationships you already have, or have had, you are fighting years of ingrained behaviors and triggers. This means that when you begin focusing on where you have no boundaries, you may begin to justify why, or come up with situational excuses as to why not, or how putting a personal boundary in that particular scenario will scare you.

Embrace all of it. Accept all of it. And then begin to build workarounds. You cannot implement healthy boundaries—and heal yourself—if you are not aware of your emotions, flaws, and reasons why certain things have been avoided. However, growth comes from discomfort, and you need to face those parts of yourself in order to grow.

Good news is that these workarounds can often be simple and easy to intuitively figure out when you remember that a boundary is what you are willing to accept, or not. If you are still unsure, keep reading, and find a safe person or professional (such as a counselor or therapist) to help you figure out what you specifically need going forward.

Others

When it comes to recognizing your boundaries—or not, as the case may be—in other relationships, we are going to look at two main categories: preexisting relationships and new relationships.

Pre-Existing Relationships

If you are someone who has no boundaries, instilling them into preexisting relationships may be a bit harder than with newer and fresher relationships. This is partly because you will be working on fixing habits within yourself *and* within that relationship. It takes two people to make a relationship, and just like your lack of boundaries did not help, their lack of boundaries, or at least boundary awareness, was just as much of a drain on the relationship.

Even if a codependent or narcissistic person is willing to attempt implementing healthy boundaries into their relationships, there will still be years of ingrained behaviors, particularly in regard to boundaries, that both parties will have to fix. A few examples of these could be:

- Ignoring your personal boundaries in favor of their own, or ignoring their own boundaries for yours

- Not understanding when there is a healthy "no," and that your affection/attention is not related to that "no"

- Not being able to have healthy, in-depth, personalized discussions without the use of guilt or manipulation tactics

Once you have recognized what the specific person's reaction to healthy boundaries are (which could be any of the above scenarios, or a few others), it is time to begin bringing realization, acknowledgement, and new healthy boundary-based habits and mindsets into your relationship.

Remember: these tips are for you, particularly for you moving forward. These are not necessarily things that are meant to save your current relationship with a codependent or narcissistic person, but they can be used for that.

New Relationships

Good news is that even if you are a budding boundaries person, newer relationships will take less effort on your part, to begin putting healthy boundaries in place. Since this is a new relationship, neither you, nor the other person, will be incredibly aware of each other's boundaries right away. Meaning that there will be time for you to get to know the person, and their boundaries, as you maybe are figuring out your own within that relationship. You also will not be fighting old habits from a bad relationship with bad boundary habits.

However, this does not mean that you are 100% in the clear. You will still have to struggle and be aware of your own boundaries and perhaps your own ingrained reactions to having to instill boundaries on your own. This means that there may be times when you feel like you are being selfish, or that you are making the other person feel like a bad friend, or that you do not want to be their friend anymore.

Good news is that, if you ever feel that way, most people will not be offended, upset, or even necessarily annoyed, when you ask to confirm your feelings. As long as it is not often or consistent. If you need a little bit more affirmation with the person that your boundaries are not getting in their way, or necessarily making you into the bad guy, you can always be upfront with them and tell them that you are learning how to have a healthy relationship, and you may ask or check-in with them about boundaries a little bit more than normal.

While you can always ask, you also have to be prepared for what might be one of your biggest fears: the truth when it hurts. There may be times when you think you are doing an amazing job of keeping boundaries and being respectful, when the other person in the relationship will tell you otherwise. When this happens, it will sting. It will hurt. But, how you handle this hurt– and how the other person tells you and handles you right afterwards–will be a good indicator if this is a good relationship for you.

Even when someone gives you criticism, they should do it in a loving and caring way. Meaning that they should not make you feel more guilty than you most likely already are, and they should not be putting more blame on you than necessary. On the other hand, you also have to hear their criticism without becoming insecure, argumentative, or confrontational. Just as you have the right—and they have likely given you permission—to check in about your boundaries; they also have the right to tell you when you actually are not respecting their boundaries or being consistent with yours. Or, they also have the right to tell you that they do not want to do constant check-ins, but want to still be friends.

You cannot be upset when your boundaries are not what someone is capable of, or looking for. If someone is willing to be a guiding hand with you on this journey, great! They are above and beyond a good friend (as long as a different safe person also believes that they have good boundaries). But if someone is not as willing because they are not comfortable with you like that, yet (remember, this is most likely a new relationship), you cannot be upset. You have to accept that. Because that is their boundary. Yes, this boundary is fluid and could change overtime, but right now, that is where they are at. And just like you want them to respect your boundaries, you also have to respect theirs.

Small Note

Yes, this was a big hullabaloo about how boundaries in new relationships work. But, while some people are more than willing to be helpful as a friend, they most likely are not always willing to sign on to be an accountability partner or a safe person. If you begin putting them into those roles and you recognize it, you need to either ask them if they are willing to take that on, or stop.

Additionally, this is a new relationship, you may not want to burden them with this kind of stuff right away. If this is you, how you are feeling, or anything like that, but you still want to learn how to implement your boundaries in a healthy way, ask a different safe person—or hire a therapist—to help you on this journey.

There are many ways to begin implementing your boundaries in a healthy way, into a new relationship. But since you are not accustomed to that just yet, having a helping hand somewhere in the mix is not a bad idea.

Re-Adapt

If you have been in long-term relationships with any type of person who has never had, or insisted, on personal healthy boundaries within the relationship, it is going to feel weird, alien, and even mean or cruel to you at times.

Why?

Because you are finally standing up for what you want, not wavering when challenged, and beginning to accept that other people's reactions to your boundaries are not your problem. That does not mean you should be rude, or put your boundaries ahead of other people's selfishness.

Consider the example:

Kate is part of a close-knit friend group, and she enjoys the bond she shares with each person. However, the person people would call her "best friend," Jake, tends to put Kate's needs above his own, to the point where other people have teased them about it. While on the surface, it all seemed fine, overtime, Kate began to get uncomfortable. Jake would constantly try to put Kate's needs above everyone else's at group outings, insisting that she get whatever she wanted. Not only was that incredibly awkward, but this somehow enabled Jake to become overly attached to Kate. He had started inviting himself over to her apartment, to events outside of their friend circle. She felt like she was suffocating and never had time to herself or one-on-one time with other friends. But, even as she got more and more frustrated, Kate let Jake be, because she knew it would hurt his feelings if she said anything. Plus, he was not really "harming" her, or anything.

Before comparing this to the healthy boundary example, let's discuss why this particular scenario is not healthy. First, Jake put Kate's needs above his own to the point where it was noticed by others. When we are good friends with someone, and if they are going through a hard time, or if that is our love language, we will often put their needs above our own the majority of the time. Or, we will sometimes be overly accommodating. Depending on your personality, love language, and history with that friend, that may be normal. However, Jake did this to the point where their friend group teased them about it; meaning that this was above and beyond what normal friends would do for each other. Secondly, Kate was getting uncomfortable. Even when you are trying to be a "healthy" pleaser, when the other person gets uncomfortable, that normally is a good indicator that you are still going too far (outside of very specific circumstances). Additionally, Kate never felt like she could actually speak up with how uncomfortable she was getting. The minute someone feels like they cannot tell someone they are upset, there is a breach or miscommunication of boundaries.

Third, Jake becomes overly attached to Kate, to the point where we start to see him isolating her, due to his own need to see her all the time. Kate was missing seeing other friends without Jake, and Jake was putting himself into her close-boundary scenarios, without asking.

Fourth, and arguably most important, Jake never let Kate feel like she could tell him to stop without feeling guilty. While the devil's advocate could say that that is a Kate problem, for the sake of this example, let's say that that is not the case.

Fifth, Kate was beginning to accept Jake's lack of boundaries by reminding herself that this did not present as normal abuse.

When you feel smothered and guilted into constantly hanging out with someone, to the point where you have to justify *their* actions *to yourself* by saying that, "Everything is alright," something is not alright.

Intrinsically, many of us have and are aware of our personal boundaries—even when we grow up in situations without them, or healthy representations of them—the problem is that over time we continue to squash that little voice inside us to the point where it often will not speak up anymore, which just continues the cycle.

Re-Introduce

There is no point in sugarcoating it; re-introducing boundaries will be hard. You are forcing yourself to do things you most likely found uncomfortable a few months ago, and certainly never thought of doing. But in order for you to grow and form healthier relationships, this is what it takes. It will be hard because you will be fighting your own insecurities just as much as the other person will be; and then on top of that, you both will have to work together to create and maintain the new and healthy boundaries going forward.

If that sounded daunting and like it would be too much work, ask yourself if you want to keep this relationship. Because overtime, as you begin to form new and healthy boundaries in other relationships, the unhealthy and lack of boundary relationships will become more annoying, painful, and hard for you to be in.

That being said, do not let that stop you! If there is a relationship you really want to keep, but you both need to work on boundaries, bring that up with the person. If they are accepting and willing to work on their boundaries, and therefore on the boundaries of the relationship, with you, then you really lucked out on an amazing person!

For example, remember Kate from the previous section? What if she confronted Jake and they decided to work on their boundaries in the relationship together?

After a while, Kate decided to talk to Jake. She had had enough; while she still wanted his friendship, she did not want him constantly inviting himself into her personal space. She asked him to meet for coffee, and then told him plainly—but nicely— how she felt, and what she needed from him. "Jake," she said, after a sip of coffee, "I want you to know, before going any further, that I still want you as a friend, and I respect your needs and wants. But I need you to be more aware of my personal space and relationships with other people. Over the past few months we have been hanging out a lot more—which on the one hand, I love—but on the other, you are not letting me have time to myself or with other friends." After taking a few minutes to digest what Kate had said, Jake clarified a few things, including asking for examples. Jake told Kate his reasons/emotions/thoughts for doing those actions, and together they were able to isolate Jake's needs in their relationship. Having established what both of them needed, Kate and Jake began to think of and make workarounds for those scenarios, so that together, they could form healthy boundaries in their relationship.

A Few Things About Boundaries

Yes, this chapter has a lot to say, but that is because

codependent and narcissistic relationships thrive on a lack of personal boundaries, so it is incredibly important you understand all the finite details about them, so that you are able to build a healthy boundary radar for current and future relationships.

They Are Tricky

Meaning that you have to know that personal boundaries are a little bit tricky. You may not always get it right the first time, you may make mistakes. And that is okay. Learning and figuring out—and admitting when you are wrong—is actually a big part of boundaries. It helps you begin to build that radar-like sense of when something is healthy and when something is wrong.

They Are Fluid

Personal boundaries are fluid, with personal exceptions like: touch, respect, time, etc., but even then, those boundaries can be fluid. Why? Because our personal relationships are always constantly changing: They are the perfect definition of fluidity. And inflicting strict, rigid, and unbending boundaries on those types of relationships is not healthy and becomes a bit dictatorial.

Small Note

There are some exceptions to this: essentially anything that will cause you to regress in your personal boundary journey, puts you or someone else in harm or danger, or is at the cost of someone else's boundaries or safety.

For instance, if you are a recovering alcoholic, your boundary of not being near alcohol is what is (presumably) keeping you sober and in a good place. This is a perfectly okay boundary.

What is not okay is when you insist everyone abstain in front of you. If you were at a friend's outdoor backyard and you insisted that you can only come if nobody else drinks, you are putting your personal boundary and need onto people who may not even know you. And if the tables were reversed, would you be okay with that? Most likely not.

This is also a great example of how boundaries are so fluid, even when they are rigid and exacting to us personally. The best way to live and cope with that is to figure out workarounds, or very good forms of communication.

They Will Be Different

This almost goes without saying, but just in case: many of your boundaries are going to be different based on the person/atmosphere/situation. A great example is how you have different personal boundaries about personal touch in your social/personal life compared to your professional one. You may hug your close friends or new acquaintances, but you most likely do not hug your coworkers.

Technically, these are different boundaries, however they do fall under the main concept of physical touch. Another way to look at it is that your boundaries will be different depending on the situation because they are fluid (from the previous section); and that is okay and healthy.

You need to understand these finite differences in order to maintain and have healthy boundaries in every aspect of your life. Overarching boundaries are necessary at times, but they can also sometimes be more restricting and harmful, than helpful.

Take It Slow

This may seem a bit odd, since boundaries are a cornerstone to healthy relationships, but think about it for a minute. Anything worth doing, is worth doing well and correctly the first time (obviously it will take several tries, but you get the idea). This is incredibly important in boundaries. Mostly because they often involve relationships with other people. While you can technically change them as you go, if you change them too frequently and often, you may actually give the wrong impression and lose people's respect and attempts to follow and obey your boundaries, rather than maintain relationships that honor them.

That being said, we all have several big personal boundaries that can always be maintained. These include: what kind of physical intimacy/touching we allow in all our relationships (they do not have to be the same in each one), how we let people talk to us or respect us, how we handle other people, and what we expect in regards of respect (such as: time, cleanliness, and words).

However, there are so many other boundaries we all figure out as we go. Such as: how much you are going to tell someone the closer you get to them, if you are going to continue being super professional or ease into the team atmosphere a little bit more, etc. Those types of fluid boundaries are completely okay to figure out on a case by case basis, and often, these will not need in-depth communication as you go. You may actually notice that you pick things up rather quickly and begin to not even notice when you are using your healthy boundaries consistently.

Final Thoughts

This chapter was a lot to take in, so here is a checklist of a few things to remember as you go forward with implementing boundaries in relationships, both new and old:

- Acknowledge what is actually your responsibility and what is not.

- Look at your life and relationships: begin to identify where you will have problems implementing these boundaries.

- Get an accountability partner or mentor if needed.

- Brainstorm and think about what types of boundaries you can implement in the areas you noticed you did not have any.

- Slowly begin implementing your boundaries over time.

- Remember that this is for you, your own good, and your mental health.

CHAPTER 7

The Art of Learning to Live and Love Again

So far in this book we have covered a lot of ground in identifying and understanding: codependent and narcissists in relationships, negative thinking and its harm to any type of relationship, the beauty of interdependence, and how to find and instill strong relational boundaries. Now it is time to begin taking everything that has been discussed and compress it into actionable goals.

In this chapter, we are going to use your newfound knowledge to begin teaching yourself how to live and love again, whether that be in a completely new relationship, or how to feel safe and secure in your old/current one with a changing and evolving partner.

Learning to live and love again, is in fact, an art. It is an art because you are starting over; and that is never an easy task. No matter how it looks, whether it is a new relationship, or re-making an old one; it is hard. You are personally unlearning large amounts of unhealthy habits, disarming traumas, and trying to instill new knowledge and coping mechanisms to be healthy. You might already know this, but it needs to be said: some days are going to be great, and some are going to be overwhelming. Both are normal and expected. It is okay for you to have days where even the concept of living and loving normally again are too much. When you have one of those days, feel free to rest, do the bare minimum, or save your emotional energy and support for yourself and chosen loved ones. Not everyone needs all of you every minute of every day.

You have gone through a lot, and you are going to continue going through a lot as you re-examine and rework old habits and mindsets. But on those hard days, do not give into the feelings of just existing or doing nothing. Take time when you need it, rest when you need it, but do not give up. You are so close to the good stuff and being "normal" again (or perhaps obtaining normal for the first time ever). With that being said, it is time to get into the exact things you need to do to begin living and loving again.

When overcoming something and then learning how to restart your life, emotions, and actions, there are generally four stages that you have to go through: acceptance and forgiveness, removing the victim, overcoming resistance, and setting goals.

Acceptance and Forgiveness

When you are leaving a bad place, it is almost easier to completely ignore what has happened and live like you have amnesia about that period of time. But that is actually way more harmful than you could imagine. Living in chosen ignorance will ensure that you continue bad habits, bad relationships, and let that previously negative situation happen again.

Whereas, if you begin to practice the art of acceptance and forgiveness towards yourself, you will be able to begin moving forward. Why? Because practicing acceptance and forgiveness actually instigates the process of beginning to grieve the past. It may not seem like it, and it certainly is not a great part to experience, but grieving is actually the beginning of moving past whatever it is that happened. The problem is that this particular step looks different for everyone, and is chosen to be ignored by many.

Ignoring and refusing to accept and forgive yourself is a surefire way to have a convoluted healing process. You are never going to be able to foster healthy relationships with other people if you do not have a healthy one with yourself. Now there is a fine line between accepting and forgiving the ugly parts of yourself and perhaps being too comfortable with them. For instance, if you just came out of a codependent relationship, it is completely acceptable to still mentally cringe when you remember that relationship, but not beat yourself up about it. It is another thing entirely to be at ease with the knowledge that you were in that relationship, and feel perfectly justified in not worrying about the cause and effect it had on you.

Accepting and forgiving is basically stating, "This is uneasy for me to remember, but I choose to forgive myself/others for my/their actions" *consistently*. Additionally, part of that forgiveness is actually not dwelling on it consistently. You can be aware that it happened. You can avoid similar circumstances. And it is really encouraged that you learn from that scenario. However, if you mentally keep thinking about it years down the road, then you have not really experienced forgiveness towards yourself or others in that situation. You have created this weird, pseudo-forgiveness, hostage-like "situationship."

Now, to be clear: Any type of trauma you have experienced is never going to go fully away. You are always going to have flashbacks, bad memories, or perhaps some type of worry/anxiety that it can happen again. That is normal. Hopefully, they become fewer and less frequent. And these instances are definitely not a sign that you have not *not* forgiven someone. If, however, you are able to fight the trauma and live a relatively easy life in relation to that trauma, and still choose to be bitter, then there is a problem with how you believe forgiveness works.

Consider the following example:

Mark and Abigail broke up over five years ago. Admittedly, the breakup was not a good one. It was messy, friends and family got involved and it resulted in Abigail completely abandoning the friend group and going on a different life path. The two attempted to reconcile early on in the breakup, but for multiple reasons, it did not take. Fast forward to five years later. Mark is married with a child and Abigail is a happy professional. Both are seemingly happy, and while they have friends in common, they have not spoken since the attempted reconciliation. It appeared that both sides were genuinely content with their lives and would probably be polite if ever in the same setting, but neither were going to go out of their way to make that happen. However, when Abigail's name comes up in context as a potential love interest for a mutual friend, Mark goes out of his way to mention how she is not as mature as she seems—due to her choice to not respond to a message on social media he had sent a few months ago—and was adamant that her actions were proof of immaturity. In comparison, Abigail barely thought about Mark until that said message popped up. After talking about it with a few chosen safe people, she chose not to respond and block Mark on all social media platforms.

In this example, Mark and Abigail appeared to have reached a relatively happy level of forgiveness, but still wanted distance (this is normal). However, Mark's actions of going out of his way to bad-mouth Abigail in a situation that had no viable reason to affect him, shows that what he considers forgiveness, is not bringing the same level of healing as Abigail's.

If you have just come out of a relationship—or are still in one with a recovering codependent or narcissist—the above example of James and Abigail may seem a little hard to relate to. So let's break it down.

Just like with Mark and Abigail, you are allowed to feel hurt and resentment immediately after a messy break-up, or during an argument with a significant other. You need to experience those feelings. However, over time, you need to be able to return to those feelings with hindsight and awareness in order to accept what is your fault, forgive yourself for your own actions, and then move on.

For those of you who think that it is either impossible to complete this step, or that you can skip it: each of these steps will take time. It will take a while, and a lot of active consistent actions on your end, to actually "complete" these steps. Because for these steps, completion is going to look like Abigail's side of the breakup: You do not even notice your will to complete the follow-through anymore.

So, yes, these steps can be combined while you do the work. However, if you do not do the work, sooner or later, you will slip into old habits and negative thoughts which in turn, could allow you to go back to toxic and negative relationships. You need to do the work, even when it might seem like you are not.

Removing the Victim

The next step is to remove any sense of victimhood from both you and your partner. Yes, you may have had victim moments, but the minute you continue—or even begin to feel entitled to—the label of "victim," you are no longer in a cooperative place to try and be helpful to save, or at least mend, the relationship; let alone actually begin to heal yourself.

Go back to the previous example of Mark and Abigail. After Mark reached out on social media—remember, the two have had no contact for years at this point—Abigail needed a few days to be upset. This is normal and viable. The length of time is not prescribed, and it might take awhile for someone to fully understand, acknowledge, and get over something that has happened to them. However, unlike Mark, Abigail let the moment pass and she continued on with her life.

In comparison, Mark went out of his way to bad mouth Abigail to mutual friends, he ensured that his two cents (which were incredibly negative and from a place of victimhood) were heard. After a breakup, someone is almost always a victim. However, when you are no longer in that relationship—and have in fact, moved onto another, more permanent one—that previous sense of victimhood (outside of extreme abuse, which would require therapy) is no longer viable or acceptable.

Honestly, at some point in time, the majority of us have been victims in one situation or another. While unfortunate, it is completely feasible to be upset or feel a need to justify why you are upset in those moments. This is normally because we are victims due to someone else's feelings of superiority or complete disregard of social etiquette or niceties (yes, this is an incredibly broad view, but go with it for now). In each of those circumstances, the victim has to acknowledge that they are a victim, but still move forward in order to be productive in that environment.

The same for here.

Being in a relationship with a codependent or narcissistic person can absolutely mean that you have been victimized. There is no denying that. At all. And that is certainly not what this book is saying.

However, if you truly want to fix and save things, you have to find a way to let your feelings of being a victim be acknowledged and then drop it. When we continue to insist that our victimization needs to be validated by everyone in our circle outside of that relationship—maybe even to strangers—we leave the circle of victimhood into a weird combination of victim and vengeance. Sounds weird, but it is kind of true. Whether you know or are aware of it or not, the minute you need validation from multiple people about the situation (or essentially to agree with you that you have been mistreated) you are either a victim of extreme gaslighting/abuse (in which case, find a safe person and get out of there), or you are ignoring how being a victim actually works. Please note that needing validation or confirmation of being a victim from a safe person(s) or counselor/therapist does not count.

Being a victim intrinsically means that you were tricked or deceived in that particular scenario; and you very well might have been. However, the minute you need to adamantly get everyone to believe your story—or even prove to your previous abuser that you are better than ever—it leaves the realm of victimhood into the concept of vengeance or retribution.

Honestly, retribution for a serious wrong makes a lot of sense. Yet our world is unjust, and often the type of justice a lot of people want simply no longer applies or is perhaps a bit too harsh for modern society. Additionally, once you have reached that place of victimhood-vengeance, you are no longer going to be open or willing to have an honest dialogue with yourself, or your partner.

Which ties into the previous section: Part of being able to accept and forgive a scenario is to actually remove the victim from the equation. This does not mean that you have to ignore, or not acknowledge, the victim moments or situations you have gone through. What this means is that you have to begin being honest with yourself and your partner. Part of that is acknowledging and communicating the situations where you were the actual victim.

However, the other part is to actually begin taking responsibility for your choices in certain moments, or situations. This step is perhaps one of the hardest—and most ignored—part of actually beginning to create a healthy love relationship and life. It is not enough to acknowledge and accept where you were a victim: you have to also begin noting where you went wrong in some situations leading up to, or in, that.

This may be a lot to digest, so let's walk it through a little bit.

Acknowledging when you are a victim is needed, because you may be trying a little too hard to accept that things have gone wrong. Once you have acknowledged that, you need to then accept that the situation and relationship has happened to you, which will allow you to move on and begin to accept and forgive yourself in letting that scenario happen at all. Then, we come to the main facet of removing the victim label from the situation and beginning to take responsibility for our own choices. This could be recognizing where you allowed certain behaviors to happen, did not speak up, or let someone make a decision for you. Either way, once you begin to realize that there are some actions you are accountable for, it is time to move onto the next step.

Overcoming Resistance

When you have begun to actively attempt to remove the victim from your situation through open communication and acknowledging your own mistakes, you can then begin to combat the resistance that you have met through any, and all, of these steps.

For instance, did you know that codependents often mask their feelings of discomfort through the use of medicated, or not, drugs, and/or technology and social media? Often when we are uncomfortable—and are not willing to acknowledge or combat it—we begin to create resistance habits to those feelings. Over time, those feelings become subconscious, or maybe conscious, triggers to start doing something else that will cause our brains to become distracted and forget about its original mission.

Codependents are not the only ones who do this. This particular habit can happen with anyone. For instance, did you ever try to have an open and honest talk with a codependent partner, friend, or spouse, but because it was an uncomfortable topic, they mentally and emotionally checked out? Or, did the opposite happen where you checked out because you were uncomfortable? That, right here, is the resistance we are trying to overcome.

A lot of us do these types of things, especially if we grew up in unhealthy scenarios of conflict. We develop these little ticks and triggers to help get our brains off of the feeling of overwhelming and upcoming doom. And it is a hard trigger to work through. Mostly because we are then forcing our brains to leave a zone of comfort which was created in the face of adversity, to then actually face the adversity or conflict.

No one likes conflict, but it is even worse in people who have unhealthy relationships with it.

Which then brings up questions on how you can begin overcoming resistance, or, on a larger scale, how to begin loving again after your previous relationship. Now it is time for us to turn to these tactics and begin exploring them, so that you are fully confident on how to properly overcome them in the present and future.

Set Goals

When it comes to setting goals there are two aspects you have to consider. The first is actually identifying your goals and figuring out how you are going to achieve them. The second is actually problem solving. Utilizing problem solving while attaining your goals will help you get there more quickly, as well as ensure that your ability to understand how to achieve your goal is done properly without avoiding uncomfortable situations.

Setting Goals

Setting goals may seem like an odd thing to have here, especially since most of these talks and tricks are referring to ways to get a healthier romantic relationship or love life. But just like how some couples set the goal of dating to get married, setting goals for yourself within the relationship is not necessarily a bad thing. Plus, with the use of CBT, and/or the help of a therapist, you will be able to incorporate all the work required to set goals easily and consistently. Remember in the previous chapter how we discussed that CBT was goal-oriented? This is where the two concepts come into alignment.

Using CBT with your therapist will help you begin to identify what goals you want to achieve, while also giving you the specific tools you will need to complete the job. Additionally, they will give you the ability to begin distinguishing between short and long-term goals, which in our lives and relationships, are wonderful and necessary skills to have.

Setting goals will also help you begin to focus on the process as much as the outcome, which in turn, will help you be able to get through those hard days where the effort required to actually reach your goal may seem like too much.

When setting your goals do not forget that you need to break them down. Goals come in pieces and bits, meaning that you may have one big, overarching goal of sobriety, for example, but you need to break that down into little chunks in order to be successful. Or, you may only have tiny little goals, which when you put them all out onto a piece of paper could become one massive goal that will span a year or more. Regardless of where you start, you need to be aware of the time it will take to achieve these goals and realistically what kind of problems you may encounter.

Problem-Solving

Which brings us to the second aspect of setting goals: problem solving. Again, if you decide to use the CBT method, you and your therapist can come up with multiple coping mechanisms to help you begin to build and re-work your existing problem solving skills.

However, here are a few ideas to get you started.

First, you need to identify your problem. Normally these are the areas where you know that you are triggered, upset, or where you will encounter some type of difficulty. But identifying them needs to be specific. You may not know certain triggers, but if you know that certain things make you angry, anxious, upset, or put you in a headspace where you may not want to be consistent to work through it and get to your goal; that is a problem. Literally.

So, write those down. Make a list, and include the triggers that you are aware of along with the emotions that come with those problems.

Second, come up with a list of possible solutions. This could include how to handle the situation, or how to better prepare yourself so that you are more responsive than reactive to the problem.

Third, you need to then go through each solution and begin to evaluate the strengths and weaknesses of each of them. Begin to think about which ones are good ideas, but will not work for you. Also write down why they most likely will not work for you. Be really honest with yourself here. Even saying "I just do not like this one," is okay for now. You may have to use it anyway, but identifying your feelings toward a solution will go a long way in determining which will be the most effective in the immediate short-term.

Fourth is picking a solution to start with. Which is why you needed to evaluate what you could, or could not, do and how you felt about those actions. Picking something you know you will not like is just ensuring that you will fail. Unless you do not like the entire process, then you are really going to have to determine how much you want this. Sooner or later, when we are on the path of change, we are going to be uncomfortable and are going to have to do things we do not want to do. That is normal, natural, and ultimately it only gets slightly better. But if this is your first time doing this—or, if you are still healing— try to pick something that is a little easier on yourself to ensure you get the habit of consistency. While many of us do not want to hear it: starting with the smallest and not the hardest option is often the best way to ensure we gain the self-discipline to be consistent for a long enough period of time to actually begin doing the harder stuff.

CHAPTER 8

The Basics of Self-Care

It may seem like after this big spiel given in the previous chapter, that these final two chapters are only focusing on how to take care of yourself. You would be right. Why? Because if you do not take care of or love yourself, then you are not going to be fit to take care of or love other people. It sounds incredibly cliche, but it is true. Part of the reason you were in that other relationship is because you did not have the self-care, self-love, and self-awareness to immediately recognize what was going on. And that is not your fault. But now it is time for you to begin building those parts of yourself up so that it never happens again. Plus, it is amazing to see how much better we love our partners, friends, and family members when we take better care of ourselves.

Now, onto self-care. To many people, especially if you are on social media, self care looks like bubble baths, manicures, facials, and sunny walks. For some people this may be what self-care looks like; but ultimately self-care actually discusses your ability to recognize when you need time to rest and rejuvenate. This could look different for a lot of people. The key here is to begin deciphering the types of self-care you may need.

Small Note

It is so easy when we are looking for ways to cultivate our own self-care routine to begin thinking we need to try everything. Part of that is true; you need to try certain things before you decide if they are right for you. However, do not let yourself be swayed from things you intrinsically know about yourself, just because you saw it on social media or got a recommendation from a friend.

You can definitely try new things; but always make sure you are monitoring yourself to see how you feel about something afterwards.

Finding your own self-care routine can generally be broken down into the four main parts of your life: your mind, body, soul, and environment.

Your Mind

Figuring out what type of self-care your mind needs is one of the top things a lot of people actually do not always do when it comes to their self-care ritual. Part of this is because a lot of us are not entirely sure of what it looks like, or they believe that "zoning out" is good enough. Another reason is because our minds are connected to every other part of our bodies; so when we provide self-care to our emotions/soul, or our physical body, we will instantly feel it in our mind/brain. Additionally, there is no "good" or prescribed way to achieve self-care; because it is entirely tailored to you and your needs. However, here are a few suggestions from *Everyday Health*:

- Go out into nature.

- Enjoy more sunlight.

- Do something creative.

- Practice kindness and gratitude.

- Meditate.

- Take time to just sit and let your mind coast along.

- Volunteer. (DiGiulio et al., 2021)

While these things seem like they may tie into the other branches of self-care (and they might), these suggestions also incorporate aspects where your brain will be able to experience something different than simply watching the next murder-mystery show on your streaming service, or the latest videos on social media. These suggestions also get you out of your comfort zone and routine, which in turn, could give your brain another jolt out of its own routine and be able to experience and try new things.

Your Body

A lot of us are pretty attuned to when our body needs a break; and this is often where things like bubble baths, self-care manicures/facials, or even that self-care glass of wine come into play. But there are other things you could do, according to *VeryWell Mind*, including:

- Exercise.

- Eat more vegetables and fruits.

- Get more sleep.

- Drink more water.

- Try different types of exercise. (Scott, 2020)

Like with our minds, our bodies do not always need to not do anything (although that could be the case more often than not). Sometimes it just needs a little bit more of something to function a bit better, or a different type of movement to help jump out of the rut that it is in.

Thankfully, our bodies are incredibly intuitive and adaptable to whatever we try to do, so if you think laying on the couch is a good idea, but you try 10 minutes of yoga, it will most likely not be too mad at you. You may even enjoy it.

Your Soul

This may sound a little deep, but there is no denying that at some level, spiritual self-care is incredibly beneficial. This does not mean that you have to go to a religious institution or suddenly find God or whomever. What it does mean is that you are fostering and nurturing a deeper sense of meaning outside of yourself. It could mean that you spend day at a time in nature with no electronics, or that you watch the sunset every night.

We need to be reminded that there is more to this life and in this world outside of us; and as odd as it seems, remembering that fact can be incredibly centering and relaxing.

Your Environment

This section pertains to both your physical and emotional environment. You know what? Our lives are messy, and that comes up in our houses. Which is perfectly fine. However, a form of self-care can sometimes equate to keeping our physical spaces tidier and less of a mess (this may also actually help your physical self-care, especially if you are allergic to dust). Additionally, the less clutter and chores you have piled on top of your immediate area, the more your emotions and life will not feel the subtle constant reminders your space presents.

Now, this particular section needs to come with a sense of balance. Just like how it can be relaxing and wonderful to have a clean space, you need to acknowledge and recognize that parts of your life may hinder you from having the spa-like, Zen atmosphere. Pets, for instance, are constant mess makers due to their shedding and living requirements. Family, spouses, or roommates may also get in the way. So, keep these types of environmental aspects in mind when you begin to let your self-care turn to the spaces around you.

Now, for your emotional environment this is referring more so to your social life. What you let in around you will affect you. This includes your friends and the emotional energy they bring and require of you. Some days we are unable to give to anyone outside of ourselves; and that is okay. You should not be the constant giver. On the other hand, some of the people in your circle may be a constant taker, which is also not good or healthy for your self-care plans and routine.

Just remember that there is a fine line between a normal give and take relationship, versus being in a constant social drain.

In All Areas

Regardless of how your self-care looks, in all areas you need to feel heard, acknowledged, nurtured, and loved. Both by yourself and those around you. This includes them respecting when you need space to be by yourself, as well as when you want to include them on your days/journey of self-care.

Practical Tips

This chapter has a lot of explanations, so here are some practical tips to get you started.

First, create a love affair with yourself. Yes, it sounds incredibly corny, but you need to do this in order to properly begin to love again in the future. What this means is that you need to intentionally set days or times where you are taking care of yourself. During these times practice self-care, take yourself out on day-trips or dates, learn more about your own hobbies and interests.

Second, become "that" person. Use your imagination to fuel your desire to actually become the person you want to be. If you want to take that course (and can afford it), go for it. If you want

to talk to that person (and it is not dangerous or harmful to your relationship) do it. This is the time for you to be selfish. Your self-care moments/days are specifically where you can be selfish and never be ashamed of it. As long as it is not crossing or destroying someone else's boundary, or relational boundaries.

Third, be spontaneous and find laughter. It might seem weird since you were previously told to schedule time off for yourself. But, once you become used to that, do not become so regimented in your self-care that you let amazing opportunities pass you by. Take the chance, try something new, and work hard on finding the joy in the moment. It is amazing how healing both of these things can be.

Fourth, instill mindfulness. Self-care includes getting to know yourself, and while having days/times where you intentionally do that is great, you need to become mindful of yourself in all areas and situations. Mindfulness, or being more attuned to your own thoughts, feelings, and behaviors in multiple scenarios, is a good place to start.

Fifth, is self-monitor. This one comes into close proximity to mindfulness but is a little bit different. It takes years to undo a habit, and monitoring yourself either through journals or accountability partners, will keep you on the right track and act as incentive to keep going on those hard days. Additionally, it will help you become more aware of when you need an extra self-care day or few hours.

Conclusion

Understanding, deciphering, and healing from a codependent and/or narcissistic relationship is a lot of work. Hopefully by now, you are becoming a bit more aware of how much work it will actually require of you, let alone the other person. But do not let that scare you from not doing it.

Putting in the hard work, effort, and time it will take to heal from this relationship could be the difference between having a normal life and going back into the same relationship with a different name (or maybe the same name).

However, just as you have to put in the work, remember to take your time and be kind to yourself. You are dealing with a lot of trauma and will have to take the time to properly unpackage and respond to it. While you are on the road to recovery, this will not be a quick and easy fix; you should not expect that of yourself or this journey. Plus, you will have to put in the hard work to actually begin to heal.

So with our few remaining words, here are a few things to remember: You can do this, it was not your fault, and the work will be completely worth it in the end.

Thank You

Before you leave, I'd just like to say, thank you so much for purchasing my book.

I spent many days and nights working on this book so I could finally put this in your hands.

So, before you leave, I'd like to ask you a small favor.

Would you please consider posting a review on the platform? Your reviews are one of the best ways to support indie authors like me, and every review counts.

Your feedback will allow me to continue writing books just like this one, so let me know if you enjoyed it and why. I read every review and I would love to hear from you. Simply visit the link below to leave a review.

References

Beattie, M. (2022). Codependent No More: How to Stop Controlling Others and Start Caring for Yourself. In Amazon. Spiegel & Grau. https://www.amazon.com/Codependent-No-More-Controlling-Yourself-ebook/dp/B09RV3Q4FM/ref=sr_1_12?keywords=codependency&qid=1658557758&s=books&sr=1-12&asin=B09RV3Q4FM&revisionId=f83d27e8&format=1&depth=1

Better Help Editorial Team. (2022a, July 29). The Power Of Negative Thinking And How To Reverse It. Better Help. https://www.betterhelp.com/advice/general/the-power-of-negative-thinking-and-how-to-reverse-it/?utm_source=AdWords&utm_medium=Search_PPC_c&utm_term=PerformanceMax&utm_content=&network=x&placement=&target=&matchtype=&utm_campaign=17990185911&ad_type=responsive_pmax&adposition=&gclid=Cj0KCQjwgO2XBhCaARIsANrW2X3yNh56lhYqHfHOim8ZTMBw03mIs-NCknN-eXj_B2a7KovcX8aahbsaAnUdEALw_wcB

Better Help Editorial Team. (2022b, August 2). 7 Types Of Narcissists And Narcissism Traits To Look For. Betterhelp. https://www.betterhelp.com/advice/personality/7-types-of-narcissists-and-what-to-look-for/?utm_source=AdWords&utm_medium=Search_PPC_c&utm_term=_&utm_content=143540811721&network=g&placement=&ta

rget=&matchtype=&utm_campaign=17990185914&ad_type=text&
adposition=&gclid=CjwKCAjw0dKXBhBPEiwA2bmObWwxDpe
EvTHOwWWlWd3e8s7HJSIvomoK1BuQg9q0aDEvFHuOxnOmo
hoCUh4QAvD_BwE

BetterHelp Editorial Team. (2022, August 2). What Is A Narcissistic
Personality: Knowing The Signs And Symptoms? BetterHelp.
https://www.betterhelp.com/advice/personality-disorders/what-is-
a-narcissistic-personality-knowing-the-signs-and-
symptoms/?utm_source=AdWords&utm_medium=Search_PPC_c
&utm_term=PerformanceMax&utm_content=&network=x&place
ment=&target=&matchtype=&utm_campaign=17990185911&ad_t
ype=responsive_pmax&adposition=&gclid=CjwKCAjw0dKXBhB
PEiwA2bmObZPRM5xXiFMBQS7tPep2mfh7XZvYzklwhj1jo969q
P1pPCZSEKxYDxoCGFQQAvD_BwE

CBT for Couples and Relationship Problems | Couples Therapy Los
Angeles. (n.d.). Cognitive Behavioral Therapy Los Angeles. Retrieved
August 2, 2022, from https://cogbtherapy.com/relationship-
problems-los-
angeles#:~:text=Cognitive%20Behavioral%20Therapy%20(CBT)%
20is

Clarke, J. (2021, July 26). Interdependence Can Build a Lasting and
Safe Relationship. Verywell Mind.
https://www.verywellmind.com/how-to-build-a-relationship-based-
on-interdependence-4161249

Cognitive Behavioral Therapy Los Angeles. (n.d.). What is Cognitive
Behavioral Therapy | About Cognitive Behavioral Therapy Los
Angeles. Cognitive Behavioral Therapy Los Angeles. Retrieved
August 4, 2022, from https://cogbtherapy.com/about-cbt

Cuncic, A. (2020, June 29). How to Change Your Negative Thought
Patterns When You Have SAD. Verywell Mind.
https://www.verywellmind.com/how-to-change-negative-thinking-
3024843

Destination Hope Blog. (n.d.). Women and Codependency.
Destination Hope Substance Abuse Treatment. Retrieved August 2,
2022, from https://destinationhope.com/women-and-

codependency/#:~:text=Some%20characteristics%20of%20codepe
ndency%2C%20according

DiGiulio, S., Millard, E., & Migala, J. (2021, October 6). Self-Care Tips During the Coronavirus Pandemic | Everyday Health. EverydayHealth.com. https://www.everydayhealth.com/wellness/top-self-care-tips-for-being-stuck-at-home-during-the-coronavirus-pandemic/

Editorial Staff. (2022, June 30). What Is Codependency Treatment? River Oaks. https://riveroakstreatment.com/relationships-and-substance-abuse/codependency-treatment/

Hammers-Crowell, J. (2019, March 20). Negative Thought Patterns and Sobriety. Safe Harbor Recovery Center. https://safeharborrecovery.com/negative-thought-patterns-sabotage-sobriety/

Kassel, G. (2022, May 1). 9 Signs You're Dating a Narcissist — and How to Deal with Them. Healthline. https://www.healthline.com/health/mental-health/am-i-dating-a-narcissist#lacking-empathy

Khoshaba, D. (2013, July 21). The Codependent Woman. Psychology in Every Day Life | a Publication by Dr. Deborah Khoshaba. http://www.psychologyineverydaylife.net/2013/07/21/the-codependent-woman/

Lantz, G. (2018, October 3). Codependency and Emotional Abuse | Psychology Today Canada. Www.psychologytoday.com. https://www.psychologytoday.com/ca/blog/hope-relationships/201810/codependency-and-emotional-abuse

LMFT, K. M. Me. (2020). The Codependency Workbook: Simple Practices for Developing and Maintaining Your Independence. In Amazon. Rockridge Press. https://www.amazon.com/Codependency-Workbook-Developing-Maintaining-Independence-ebook/dp/B086P96Z78/ref=sr_1_11?crid=3B9ZFDZ6I2XLS&ke
ywords=codependency&qid=1658556039&s=books&sprefix=code

pendenc%2Cstripbooks%2C439&sr=1-
11&asin=B086P96Z78&revisionId=f75b6eaa&format=1&depth=1

Martin, S. (2020, January 10). Why Its So Hard to End a Codependent Relationship. Psych Central. https://psychcentral.com/blog/imperfect/2020/01/why-its-so-hard-to-end-a-codependent-relationship

Mayo Clinic. (2019). Cognitive Behavioral Therapy. Mayoclinic.org. https://www.mayoclinic.org/tests-procedures/cognitive-behavioral-therapy/about/pac-20384610

Menter, J. E. (2013). You're Not Crazy - You're Codependent.: What Everyone Affected By Addiction, Abuse, Trauma Or Toxic Shaming Must Know To Have Peace In Their Lives. In Amazon (3rd edition). J2 Publishing. https://www.amazon.com/Youre-Not-Crazy-Codependent-Addiction-ebook/dp/B00CKY89VQ/ref=sr_1_16?keywords=codependency&qid=1658557758&s=books&sr=1-16&asin=B00CKY89VQ&revisionId=aa83258d&format=1&depth=1

Merriam-Webster. (n.d.-a). Definition of Codependency. Www.merriam-Webster.com. Retrieved August 2, 2022, from https://www.merriam-webster.com/dictionary/codependency

Merriam-Webster. (n.d.-b). Definition of Narcissistic. Www.merriam-Webster.com. Retrieved August 2, 2022, from https://www.merriam-webster.com/dictionary/narcissistic

Peterson, S. (2018, June 11). Effects. The National Child Traumatic Stress Network; The National Child Traumatic Stress Network. https://www.nctsn.org/what-is-child-trauma/trauma-types/complex-trauma/effects

Scott, E. (2020, August 3). 5 self-care practices for every area of your life. Verywell Mind; Verywell Mind. https://www.verywellmind.com/self-care-strategies-overall-stress-reduction-3144729

University of Concordia Health Services. (n.d.). Examples of cognitive restructuring. Www.concordia.ca. Retrieved August 18, 2022, from https://www.concordia.ca/cunews/offices/provost/health/topics/stress-management/cognitive-restructuring-examples.html

Utti, C., MA, & MFA. (2016, September 19). How to Fix an Addicted and Codependent Relationship. Willingway. https://willingway.com/fix-addicted-codependent-marriage/

Villines, Z. (2018, August 7). Codependency and Narcissism May Have More in Common Than You Think. GoodTherapy.org Therapy Blog. https://www.goodtherapy.org/blog/codependency-narcissism-may-have-more-in-common-than-you-think-0807187#:~:text=People%20with%20codependency%20sometimes%20form

Wiley, C. (2020, March 3). Is There a Difference Between Narcissism and Confidence? - Talkspace. Mental Health Conditions. https://www.talkspace.com/mental-health/conditions/articles/narcissism-vs-confidence-definition-what-is/